FROM GRANNY WITH LOVE

BOOK ONE

CONFESSION
AND
FIRST HOLY COMMUNION

NICOLE HALL

Printed for the Author by
From Granny with Love

First Published in Great Britain in 2009 by
'From Granny with Love'
Not-for-Profit Division of
Peter R M Hall & Co Ltd
www.fromgrannywithlove.com

Copyright © 2009 'From Granny with Love'
Not-for-Profit Division of
Peter R M Hall & Co Ltd

ISBN: 978-0-9564026-0-8

Cover design by: Tony Kitzinger, London

Printed in Great Britain by the MPG Books Group, Bodmin and King's Lynn

Acknowledgements are given in an Appendix for those pictures which have been included by the kind permission of the copyright holder.

To:

Cecily

Agnes

Sebastian

Elisabeth-Rose

and

Felicity

TABLE OF CONTENTS

Table of Contents - continued

PREFACE

Nicole Hall has written a guide to the faith for growing children, which is filled with all her warmth, intelligence and devotion. It is the kind of guide, which can only come from living the faith and loving it over a long period of years.

What she has to say about first Confession and first Holy Communion is soaked through with good sense about how to receive these sacraments with spiritual fruit. It repays reading by those who are not children themselves, for it blows away the cobwebs which gather with the passing of time and the dulling effects of routine. Those cobwebs conceal from us the simplicity of our basic relation with God, and the directness of our Lord's presence to us as Saviour and intimate Friend. I am sure that any child who has got the message of these pages will never forget it.

Nicole has a true talent for story-telling, and we first encounter this in her recounting of the lives of the saints. She is not afraid to include and even emphasise the miraculous. We forget the real dimensions of the generosity of God: the miracles worked by the saints, either in their lifetimes or through their intercession since, are the way Grace has of forcefully reminding us, for, as Nicole writes, Grace is 'the life of God'. All nature is a gift of God, but the supernatural is his most glorious gift, because it is the invitation to share his life.

I am certain that *From Granny with Love* will do much good for souls.

Grandmothers have often been key figures in passing on the faith to a new generation. They are, often, like our Lady in the years after Pentecost. With their active work largely done, they have the opportunity to dispense the wisdom they collected, and to do so in a motherly way.

I wish *From Granny with Love* a very wide circulation.

Aidan Nichols, O. P.

Dom Fernando Arêas Rifan

Administração Apostólica Pessoal
São João Maria Vianney
Campos, RJ, Brasil

BLESSINGS

It is with pleasure that I give my episcopal blessing to the distinguished writer of this book, the "strong woman" Mrs Nicole Hall, to her kind husband Mr. Peter Hall, her mother Josée Turle, their two children Dominic and Amanda with their spouses, Alice and Ralph, their grandchildren Cecily, Agnes, Sebastian, Elisabeth-Rose, and Felicity, newly arrived sister to Cecily and Agnes. Also to her cousins Patrick, Andrew and Jane and their children and grandchildren.

May God bless and guard under his protection this good family.

+ Bishop Fernando Areas Rifan

Apostolic Adminstrator

Campos - Rio de Janeiro - Brazil

London, August 31st, 2007

INTRODUCTION

This book was written especially for my grandchildren: Cecily and Agnes Perry Robinson, Sebastian and Elisabeth-Rose Hall, and the baby Felicity, just born to Amanda and Ralph, sister to Cecily and Agnes. Also of course for any other children who might be born to my children, Dominic and Amanda after my death.

It is offered as well to my cousins, Patrick, Jane and Andrew, to their children and grandchildren.

Finally, it is for all children who might enjoy a Granny's view of our Faith.

The thought behind these books is that this explanation of Catholic teaching, on such an important subject, by their Granny may be of use to my grandchildren as they grow up, and even when they have children of their own.

As I had the great fortune to be educated at a time in the Church's history when the Faith was strong, it would also seem right to pass on what was so well passed to me, and to try to contribute, if possible, to the Faith of future generations. It has also been suggested that Grannies could well be the best channels or agents to pass on the faith to today's rising generation, because so many of their parents have been lost to the Church.

What began as a simple introduction to the First Confession and First Holy Communion of my grandchildren has just grown and grown.

I am most indebted to all those people who have helped me, principally my husband Peter, who has supported this project from the beginning, proof read for me, and is organizing the publishing, and my mother, Josée Turle, who at the age of eighty-nine has done some research for me.

This book would never have been written but for the encouragement and the teasing humour of my old friend and parish priest, Father Bernard Davenport, who suggested the title. He faithfully read each section, immediately it was produced, and provided valuable and at times quite pithy comments.

I am also greatly indebted to my Final Readers, Mrs Francis Phillips and Mrs Mary Carey for so generously devoting much precious time giving meticulous attention to detail.

My very dear friend and spiritual director, Dom Gerard of Le Barroux, was intending to write the Preface, but he died suddenly on 28th February 2008 R.I.P. He is, I am sure, guiding this little project from above. I hope to include this remarkable story later in this series.

Dom Aidan Nichols O.P., another old friend, very kindly stepped into the breach at the last moment and agreed to write the Preface, for which he has my most grateful thanks.

Many other people helped along the way and my gratitude for their various contributions is given under 'Acknowledgements'.

Nicole Hall

MY DEAR CHILDREN

My Dear Children, not just those of my own family, for whom this book was specially written, but any others, who may in the future read this book.

This book is for you to enjoy, and to use however you want to. You could also refer to it at any time in your life.

My friend, Father Hugh Thwaites S.J., has said that many families in this country have been Catholic for over a thousand years. We do not know exactly how long the Catholic Faith, founded by Jesus Himself, has been in our family. It could even be longer than a thousand years.

It comes to us partly through the French side. France is known as 'The Oldest Daughter of the Church', as on Christmas night 496 the Frankish leader Clovis, who had for so long resisted the Faith, was baptised with all his soldiers.

On the Italian side, it comes from my great grandmother, which could even predate this. However long it is exactly, the Faith has been passed down to us through each generation for very many centuries.

At Sports Day at school you have a Relay Race. One person runs across the field holding a baton, which they hand on to the next person, who takes it and runs back across the field to hand it on to the next, and so on.

The Faith is rather like this. The field is our own life, and we pass on the 'baton' of this Faith to our children, and to anyone else, who would like to know about Jesus. It is a great gift, which we have been given freely and should freely give.

As St Paul says:

> I have received of the Lord, that which also I have delivered to you.

So, I hope you will in your turn pass on St Paul's 'baton' to the children of your families, when you are grown up, so that they in turn can pass it on.

You might even like to add bits to the book yourselves; for example there are so many wonderful saints that could be included under the Story Section.

I hope that this book helps you to understand the teaching of the Church. If you follow this teaching of Jesus, the Faith will support you throughout your life, in the hard times as well as the easy times.

May you learn to know, love and serve God in this world and be happy with Him forever in the next, and may the Catholic Faith be the joy for you that it has always been for me.

God bless you all.

From Granny with Love

Plate 1: Jesus, I am Sorry for my Sins

YOUR FIRST CONFESSION

**also known as
'The Sacrament of Penance'
or of
' Reconciliation'**

Chapter 1

CONFESSION AND YOUR SOUL

So you are going to make your first Confession! That means that you are going to receive forgiveness for your sins from Almighty God Himself!

Up to now, when you have been naughty you have said 'sorry' and been forgiven, usually by Mummy and Daddy.

The Church thinks you are now grown-up enough to understand that every sin which we commit offends not only those we hurt on earth, but also offends our Father who is in Heaven. He made us, and we are all His beloved children.

So, the Sacrament of Confession is wonderful, because it brings us the forgiveness of our Eternal Father.

In this way, you are about to take your first step in your own spiritual life. This is a journey through life, in the sight of God. At the end of that journey, when you die, if you have loved God and obeyed His Church, you will go to God and live with Him in perfect joy forever.

PICTURES OF YOUR BAPTISMS

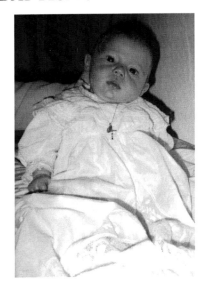
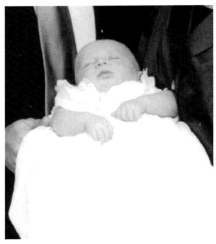
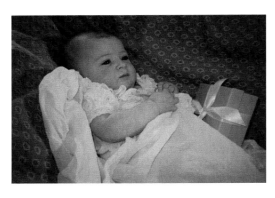
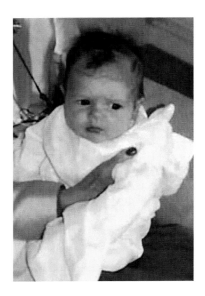

There are, as you know, seven sacraments in the Catholic Church, ordained by Jesus to help us through life. When you were baptised as a baby, God's grace flooded your soul. At that time you were far too tiny to realise or remember it. So, that first 'step' was taken for you, by your parents and godparents. You can see photographs of yourselves at your baptism opposite.

Confession, then, is the very first sacrament, which we are all old enough to understand and remember. This makes our First Confession very special.

Just imagine that you are feeling tired, miserable, dirty, and uncomfortable, with a sore throat and a headache. You are trudging along a road, wishing so much that you could get home to your loving family for a hot bath and tea.

Then right in front of you there appears a gleaming white fluffy cloud reaching to the ground. You walk through it and - suddenly - you are also dazzling white, feel totally different, you feel at home and loved, so well and full of energy that you could jump for pure joy. You feel 'perfect'.

Well, it is not your body I am talking about, but your soul. That is just my way of imagining what we cannot see. I bet you can think of a better one. You cannot see your soul. But our souls are much more important than our bodies, which one day will die. Your soul is the part of you, which is like God and can never die. God gave you that precious soul before your little body was born, and you must take the greatest care of it.

Everybody, grown-ups and children, commit sins. We all do things, sometimes, which we are sorry for afterwards, because they have hurt or angered our family or friends. Of course, we can make it up to anyone we have hurt by saying we are sorry and doing something specially helpful and kind.

It is more important, though, to realise that our sins offend, or hurt, Almighty God. We need to say 'sorry' to Him, too, for the little sins we commit. These harm our soul, His precious gift to us. That is why we have the Sacrament of Penance.

Chapter 2

ABOUT SINS AND GRACE

In my day, at school, we all went to Confession every two weeks. This was not because we had done terrible things, but just for the grace the Sacrament gives.

Nowadays people do not go so often, which is a pity. I hope that in your lifetime more people will go more often to Confession, because Jesus, who loves us and wants what is best for us, gave us this Sacrament, especially for our good.

The Grace that you gained from the Sacrament of Baptism is called 'Sanctifying Grace'. To sanctify is to make holy. This is the special Grace, which makes you the child of God enjoying His very special friendship. Every sacrament adds to this. I know it is hard to understand, for grown-ups as well as for children, but by 'sanctifying grace', we mean the actual life of God in our own souls. What a thought!

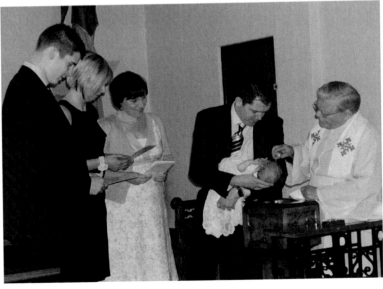

Plate 2: Baptism

All the other countless ways in which God helps us on the road to heaven are forms of what we call 'actual grace'. So, for example, without 'actual grace' it would be impossible for anyone who had rejected sanctifying grace (by serious sin) ever to get it back, to recover God's friendship.

We are baptised as babies in order to remove 'original' sin, that of Adam and Eve, which all members of the human race inherit. There are also the 'actual' sins we all personally commit. These are called just that - 'actual' sins.

There are two kinds of 'actual' sins we can commit. Most of us only commit 'venial' or small sins, but occasionally people commit 'mortal' sins, which are very serious as they kill that special sanctifying grace of God in our souls. Mortal sins are the real baddies, like murder. If you had committed a 'mortal' sin, I think you would know it.

But, our generous God does not withhold all His grace, 'actual', remember, even from those who have committed a mortal sin. Otherwise, we would never have the grace to repent or to be sorry.

We must remember, though, that it is a serious sin to miss Mass on Sundays or Holy Days through our own fault. If we are ill or in a foreign country and cannot find the church in time then we are not guilty of sin.

If, though, you know you are just going to be away from home over a week-end, perhaps staying with a non Catholic friend, you should plan in advance, and find out the place and Mass times of the local Catholic church, and warn the friend that you will be going.

Venial sins should be confessed regularly. If we neglect the Sacrament of Penance, these 'venial' sins could lead to a habit of us not being careful of our behaviour. This in turn could make it more likely that we might commit a 'mortal' sin.

The three kinds of sin are: sins against God, sins against our neighbour (other people) and sins against ourselves. It is funny to think we can sin against ourselves, isn't it? But when we tell lies for example, we sin firstly against God, secondly against the person we lie to, and thirdly we harm and diminish ourselves by this sin, which is unworthy of us as children of God.

We should think about the kinds of sins we have committed whilst we are preparing before going into confession. Let me give you one example of each. If you spoke of God in a disrespectful way; that would be a sin directly against God. If you hurt another child, that would be a sin against your neighbour. Of course it is possible to offend a sensitive or difficult person without intending to, and in that case, you would not necessarily be offending God.

If you went off on your own in a sulk, that would be sinning against others who might be upset by your behaviour, but also it would be sinning against yourself, because it is 'selfish' behaviour, which means you are thinking only of yourself and not of others. This makes you a lesser person.

When we say our night prayers, we should for a moment remember the day and say sorry to God for anything we might have done which is unworthy of His love.

Sacraments are often described as 'outward signs', or signs we can see, of hidden things which we cannot see. We cannot of course actually 'see' our soul, or the grace, which the Sacraments give to it.

So, whilst we know very well what we are doing outwardly and can hear the words pronounced by the priest, at the same time all sorts of wonderful things are happening to us inside, which we cannot see but need to know about.

Chapter 3

JESUS GIVES US CONFESSION

In the Gospel for Low Sunday, the Sunday after Easter, we are told how Jesus appeared on the evening of His resurrection from the dead, to His disciples. The disciples were, of course, astonished and very frightened, as they had seen Him actually die on the cross, and seen Him buried.

Jesus calmed their fear, and told them gently that it really was He, whom they all knew and loved. Because He loved them He reassured them in a very simple way: He just asked them for something to eat! Then, they realised that it must really be Jesus, and were overjoyed to see Him.

Had Our Lord had anything to eat since the Last Supper three days earlier, after the agony in the garden, the pain of being beaten, scourged, crowned with thorns, made to carry a heavy cross on His wounded back, and finally crucified? The Gospels do not tell us.

Plate 3: The Last Supper - Leonardo da Vinci

Here is that part of the Gospel for Low Sunday:

> Now when it was late that same day, being the first day of the week, and the doors were shut where the disciples were gathered together for fear of the Jews, Jesus came and stood in the midst and said to them "Peace be with you".
>
> And when He had said this He showed them His hands and His side. The disciples, therefore, were glad when they saw the Lord. And He said to them again "Peace be to you. As the Father has sent Me, I also send you".
>
> And when He had said this, He breathed upon them and said to them: "Receive the Holy Spirit: whose sins you shall forgive, they are forgiven them: whose sins you shall retain, they are retained".
> (John xx: 19-23)

Retained means not forgiven. This was when Jesus instituted the Sacrament of Penance and gave this wonderful power to the priests of His Church, anywhere in the world, and across all generations to forgive sins in the name of God.

His apostles and disciples, whom Jesus made priests, were ordinary sinful people living at the time Jesus was on earth. In every generation, and also in our own day, priests are human beings. They also commit sins. They are sorry for them and have to go to Confession themselves to other priests. The same applies to bishops, even to the Pope. Because of the holiness of their calling, priests have special graces. Some priests use these graces to become the most wonderful wise and holy people - I have known many such priests.

Priests have a sacred duty before God never to tell anyone about the sins they have heard in the confessional. This duty is so binding that even the law of the country cannot force a priest to reveal what he has been told in the secrecy of the confessional.

Chapter 4

THE FORM OF CONFESSION

When I was young, whether at school or in the local parish church, you knelt in the benches, praying and trying to remember all the things you had done wrong since your last Confession. This is called an 'examination of conscience'. Our 'conscience' is how we know in our hearts what is right and wrong in the sight of God.

One way of checking what we have done wrong would be to go through the Ten Commandments, which God gave to Moses, to see if we have sinned against these laws of God.

THE TEN COMMANDMENTS

1. Thou shalt not have strange gods before me.
2. Thou shalt not take the name of the Lord thy God in vain.
3. Remember that thou keep holy the Sabbath day.
4. Honour thy father and thy mother.
5. Thou shalt not kill.
6. Thou shalt not commit adultery.
7. Thou shalt not steal.
8. Thou shalt not bear false witness against thy neighbour.
9. Thou shalt not covet thy neighbour's wife.
10. Thou shalt not covet thy neighbour's goods.

The sixth and ninth Commandments are for grown-ups, so you will not have to worry about these yet. Later on you will be taught all about The Commandments in more detail and have their meaning explained, as some are not easy to understand.

Plate 4: Moses with the Ten Commandments

For now, this short explanation may help:

1. God is telling us He alone is God; so no one else, nothing else should be worshipped as God.
2. Speak about God with reverence, and not use His name in any other way.
3. Go to church to worship God. Think of Him especially on the Sabbath (now our Sunday), avoid unnecessary work and keep the day holy.
4. Love, obey and respect our parents
5. Just what it says.
6. Grown-up people, who are married, should be faithful to that marriage and not behave towards somebody else as if they were married to that person instead.
7. Just what it says - and there are many ways of stealing.
8. Do not harm your neighbour (anyone) by telling lies about him or her.
9. Do not even want to be married to someone else's wife (or husband) because he or she belongs to somebody else and not to you.
10. Do not long to have things which belong to somebody else, because they belong to that person and not to you.

Do not even want to steal. The ninth and tenth Commandments remind us that a strong desire to do something wrong is already a sin.

After your 'examination of conscience', and when it was your turn for Confession, you went into a tiny room, which was mostly dark, with a little window in the wall opposite. There was a dim light showing the priest sitting the other side listening to your sins. So you could kneel humbly in the shadows, knowing that if you made an honest confession of all the sins you could remember, and were sorry for them, then, from the dim figure of the priest, you would hear those great and beautiful 'words of absolution' of the Church. The words of absolution are words 'absolving' us or forgiving us our sins.

Then you would know that you were completely forgiven by God for every sin you had ever committed in your whole life, even if you did not remember to confess them all.

We were taught, as you will be, to pray for the grace to make a really good Confession. Remember, also, to ask Our Lady to help you in this. When you were very little and went out to the Grotto in the garden of our home, Dormers, you used to call Our Lady 'Jesus' Mummy', and so she is. Jesus loves her very much and will always listen to her, and she also will help us throughout our lives. All we have to do is to ask her.

The manner of Confession may change, but the main parts will remain:

When you first go in, you say 'Please bless me Father, f or I have sinned'. Often, as you go in, you can hear that the priest has already started blessing you, as he hears you enter the confessional. When he has finished this prayer, you then say "It is my First Confession, Father" or "It is a month", or however long it has been since your last Confession. Then:
  - You confess your sins to God, through his priest;
  - You make an 'act of contrition' - a prayer to God, saying you are sorry;
  - You make a 'firm purpose of amendment' - decide to behave better in future;
  - The priest passes on to you the forgiveness of God through the power that Jesus gave His Church.
  - Then, when you leave the confessional, you do the 'penance' the priest gives you, which often takes the form of prayers like the Hail Mary, or the Our Father.

This is your personal and all-important 'making up' to God for your sins, by doing little extra good things, like you would to Mummy and Daddy if you knew you had been naughty and were sorry.

Here are two examples of 'Acts of Contrition,' a simple one and a slightly more complicated one, perhaps for when you are older. It is your choice:

1) 'O my God, I am so sorry to have offended you, and with the help of your Grace, I will not sin again'.

2) O My God, I am heartily sorry for having offended Thee, and I detest all my sins, because I dread the loss of heaven and the pains of hell, but most of all because they offend Thee, my God, Who art all good and deserving of my love. I firmly resolve, with the help of Thy grace, to confess my sins, to do penance, and to amend my life. Amen

The priest will say 'God bless you. Please pray for me', and you will know that the confession is over. You then walk out to say your penance and then some of your favourite prayers or make-up prayers. You will be leaving the church in what is called a 'state of grace', right in the middle of that white cloud. If you were to die at that time, you could go straight to heaven!

As explained before, the word 'retained' means not forgiven. Sins are usually forgiven, certainly children's sins. Only very, very occasionally is a sin ever retained.

But it does happen sometimes when a grown up is not sorry and means to go right on committing that particular sin. In such a case, forgiveness is not given until the priest is certain that the person is really sorry and intends never to do it again or, in other words, has a 'firm purpose of amendment'.

Otherwise everyone could just say 'sorry' and walk out without meaning it. There would be no point in that would there? I mean, if you had just said in Confession that you were sorry for being rude to Mummy, and you had already decided to go straight out there and be very rude to her again, then your Confession would not have been very honest, would it?

It is more important than anything to be honest with God, who loves you, knows you better than you know yourself, and understands your every thought.

If you have committed serious sins, which you might do when you are older, you should go as soon as possible to Confession. The Church tells us to go at least once a year.

Confession is a wonderful and consoling sacrament:

> - not just because we come out in what is called a 'state of Grace', with pure souls free of all sins, or dazzling white, if you remember my cloud idea, and blessed with God's complete forgiveness; so we can forget all about those sins and never think of them again;

> - not just because of the special graces we get from it;

> - but also because it allows us to receive the great Sacrament of the Eucharist, Holy Communion, in as worthy a state as possible. If you think of it, none of us could ever be worthy enough to receive Jesus in Holy Communion.

Chapter 5

JESUS THE GOOD SHEPHERD

We think of Jesus with many names and titles: Christ, Our Lord, The Sacred Heart, The Saviour, because He 'saved' us, Lamb of God, the Messiah, which means the 'anointed one' - the deliverer the Jews were expecting, Emmanuel, which means 'God with us' and others.

The title, which perhaps makes us think particularly of Confession, is the title of 'Jesus, the Good Shepherd'. There are many pictures of Jesus carrying back on His shoulders a sheep that has got lost. We get lost when we sin and we all need Jesus to bring us back. Good Shepherd Sunday, which reminds us that Jesus is the one Shepherd of our souls, is the second Sunday after Easter. Here we hear Jesus in the Gospel saying:

Plate 5: The Good Shepherd

I am the Good Shepherd. The good shepherd giveth his life for his sheep. But the hireling whose own the sheep are not, seeth the wolf coming and leaveth the sheep, and flieth: and the wolf catcheth and scattereth the sheep: and the hireling flieth, because he is a hireling and has no care for his sheep. I am the Good Shepherd, and I knoweth mine and mine know me, and I lay down my life for my sheep (John xx: 11).

A hireling is a man who is paid to look after the sheep so doesn't do it because he loves them, and 'I knoweth mine' means that Jesus knows his own sheep, which means us.

Often in bibles and old missals you see 'th', like 'seeth' sees, and 'scattereth' scatters, after words, because they are in old-fashioned English. You also find 'Ye' and 'Thou' for you. In some ways, old English, like Latin, because it is not our ordinary everyday language, makes the words all the more special, and reminds us that we are talking about holy things.

Handel, the composer, wrote a famous Oratorio you may have heard of, called 'The Messiah,' in which he quotes from one of the prophets, Isaiah, 'but we like sheep have gone astray'.

What Isaiah actually said was:

All we like sheep have gone astray; we have turned everyone to his own way and the LORD hath laid on Him the iniquity of us all.

'We have turned to our own way', means doing what we want and not what God wants, and the last line means that Jesus took all our sins, or iniquity, on to His own shoulders.

We all do go astray like sheep, we all sin and we need the forgiveness of God to bring us back into the arms of Jesus.

I hope your First Confession makes you very happy, and that you decide to form a habit of regular Confession throughout your life. It is up to you. Nobody else will do this for you. It is your own soul, and your job to use the sacraments Jesus gave us to help us to keep the beautiful Faith He entrusted to us.

We were all created to know, love and serve God in this world and to be happy with Him forever in the next. I will certainly pray for your First Holy Confession. Even if for any reason I am not able to be with you on the day in the church, remember I will still be with you in a very special way.

Plate 6: The Last Supper by Castagno

YOUR FIRST HOLY COMMUNION

Chapter 6

JESUS GIVES US THE BLESSED SACRAMENT

So, now you are going to make your First Holy Communion, the most wonderful of all the sacraments. This is a day you will always remember!

From the time Our Lord was on earth, the Blessed Sacrament has always been the greatest treasure of the Church.

Why is this Sacrament of Love the greatest sacrament of them all? It is so, because in Holy Communion we receive God, Himself, to be our food. Just think about that!

What is 'The Blessed Sacrament'? What does Holy Communion mean? What does 'The Real Presence' mean?

We have here a mystery so great that no grown up person on earth can fully understand it. But every Catholic needs to appreciate this, and pray for an ever-deepening understanding and love for the Blessed Sacrament throughout life.

A 'mystery' is something we are unable fully to understand. We believe through Faith, which comes to us from God.

On Maundy Thursday, the day before He died for us on Good Friday, Jesus gave us the Blessed Sacrament at the Last Supper. St Paul tells us what had been passed down to him, which he is also passing down to us. That is what the word 'Tradition' means:

Plate 7: The Consecration of the Host

I have received of the Lord, that which also I have delivered to you that the Lord Jesus, the same night that He was betrayed, took bread, and giving thanks, broke, and said: Take ye, and eat; this is my body, which shall be delivered for you, this do for the commemoration of me.

In like manner, also the chalice, after He had supped, saying: This chalice is the 'new' testament in my blood; this do ye, as often as ye shall drink, for the commemoration of me. For as often as ye shall eat this bread and drink this chalice, ye shall show the death of the Lord until He come (1 Corinthians xi: 23).

The word 'supper' can give us the wrong idea. It makes us think of a cosy snack before we go to bed.

In fact the Last Supper was a serious religious celebration. It was a very formal grown-up dinner. At the command of God, the Jews had celebrated this once a year for hundreds of years on the Pascal Feast. There were strict rules about when, where, and how the meal was to be celebrated and exactly what was eaten.

It was because of the religious importance of this formal meal to the Jews that Jesus chose to set this 'New Pasch', these New Rites, within this ritual.

It was not the meal which He told us to commemorate, or to repeat in his memory, but the new part, which He set within it. This new part forms the heart of our Mass, as we know it today.

At the Consecration in the Mass, the priest holds up a little round piece of unleavened bread and says, in Our Lord's name, the words Jesus used at the Last Supper. At that moment, by the power of God, what still looks, feels and tastes like bread, becomes Jesus Himself, body, blood, soul and divinity. His divinity means his Godhead.

This is what the Blessed Sacrament means. We have the Blessed Sacrament the moment the bread and wine become Jesus, through the power of God by the action of the priest.

Those receiving the Blessed Sacrament are receiving Jesus in 'Holy Communion'. To commune with somebody is to become very close to them.

So you will, for the first time, receive Our Lord, in Holy Communion, just as the apostles did for the first time on Maundy Thursday, over two thousand years ago. What a thought! From this day on, you will go up to the altar to receive Jesus like all the grown ups do.

Plate 8: Pope Benedict XVI gives Holy Communion

Of course, your very first Holy Communion is extremely special, but you must try to remember it and to keep the freshness and wonder of your first Holy Communion every time you receive our Lord throughout your life.

When I was at school, all of us children had our First Holy Communion at early Mass. In those days we had to fast from midnight the day before, which meant that we were not allowed to eat or drink before Mass. The girls all wore beautiful white dresses made for this great occasion, whilst the boys usually wore white shirts, ties and jackets.

The nuns at my convent invited our parents and family to this very special Mass.   Afterwards we all had a scrumptious bacon and egg breakfast together. The nuns made our families feel very welcome, so it was a really joyful occasion.

The Eucharist also means the Blessed Sacrament. The Eastern Rite Catholics use the word Eucharist for the whole of what we call the Mass. The Blessed Sacrament, which we also call the Eucharist, is the central part of our Mass.

Some Eucharistic hymns, which I hope you will know and sing regularly and which will be found in a good Catholic hymn book, are:

> Jesus gentlest Saviour
> Jesus Thou art coming
> O Bread of Heaven
> Sweet Sacrament Divine
> Soul of my Saviour
> Oh Jesus Christ Remember
> Godhead here in hiding (St Thomas Aquinas, translated by Gerard
> Manley Hopkins)
> Let all mortal flesh keep silent (Liturgy of St James)

One of the Popes once said that he who sings prays twice. A nice thought, but then I love to sing. I wonder if you will when you are older. If you do not like to sing, then nourish your Faith and love of the Blessed Sacrament by reading prayers in a missal or Catholic prayer book.

Faith needs to be looked after and used and kept bright like a silver spoon. If you put it in a drawer and leave it there forgetting it, you might lose it, and that could be a terrible life-long loss.

I will always remember my first Holy Communion, and I am sure you will always remember yours. I will pray for your First Holy Communion, and if for any reason I am unable to be with you in church, I will of course be with you in a special way, as I was for your First Confession.

Plate 9: The Crucifixion by Mantegna

Chapter 7

JESUS DIES FOR US

On Good Friday Our Lord Jesus died for us, so that our sins could be forgiven, and we could go to Heaven when we die.

Jesus suffered greatly out of love for us. He knew He was going to be betrayed, by one of His own apostles, Judas, for thirty pieces of silver. He allowed Himself to be: falsely accused; arrested; beaten; mocked; scourged (whipped), and crowned with sharp thorns, which cut into his head. He carried His heavy cross on His wounded back, and finally bled to death for us nailed to a cross.

His body was tortured for us and He shed all his blood for us. As Our Lord Himself said "Greater love than this no man hath, that a man lay down His life for his friends" (John xv: 13). We are his friends.

On the hill called Calvary, the sight of our Saviour was truly terrible. We would have been filled with horror had we been there and seen Jesus so brutally treated and shedding His precious blood for us. The shock would have been more than we could bear. We would have looked away, or even run away, as most of the disciples did. But Our Lady, Jesus' mother Mary, and our mother, was there. She stood by the cross for us. She shared in all His pain for us.

You see, Our Lord, who loves us, knows just how terrible it would have been for us all to see His crucifixion, and for this reason He made sure, the day before He was to die, that He gave us Holy Communion at the Last Supper.

This way we could continue in our lives to remember His suffering and death the next day, not in a horrifying way, but in an enchanting way, using homely things that we all know so well, like bread and wine.

So, at every Mass, through the priest, we are able to relive the offering Jesus made to His Father for our sake on Calvary, all those years ago.

This way Jesus' offering, of Himself, is continued through time and space. That means that each generation and in all parts of the world, ordinary people like us, are able to add our prayers to those of the priest, who pleads, in the place of Jesus, to God our Father for the good of the living and the dead.

We call the day Jesus died 'Good Friday' because those terrible sufferings of Jesus 'redeemed' us. The word 'redeemed' means that Our Lord bought us back from sin, and made it possible for us to go to Heaven when we die. So the death of Our Blessed Lord Jesus was for our 'good'.

We, also, have to make an effort ourselves. If we want to go to Heaven, which Our Lord made possible for us at such a price of pain, He told us that we must take up our own cross in life and follow Him. So when things do not go the way we want, we have to accept this without grumbling, and concentrate on helping other people, thinking of them and their good rather than our own, and all out of love of Jesus.

During the Consecration at Mass we should also offer ourselves to God. We should offer all we can offer, ourselves, our lives, all our problems and crosses, and also our joys, so these little things may also be offered to God the Father, and added to the one great Sacrifice of all time, that of Jesus on Calvary.

Chapter 8

GOOD FRIDAY AND MAUNDY THURSDAY

The Mass and the Last Supper are intimately connected to the Crucifixion of Jesus, His one great act to redeem us.

This 'New Pasch', the giving of His Body and Blood, that Jesus inserted into the Jewish meal of the Last Supper, unites us with His passion and death, which took place the following day. So our Mass today unites us with the passion and death of Jesus two thousand years ago.

Jesus gave us the Eucharist the day before His crucifixion, because he knew He would not be able to give Himself to the apostles the next day, because then He would be carrying His cross and dying for us. That is why He says:
My Body which shall be given up for you... (see Chapter 6).

Plate 10: The Consecration of the Chalice

St Paul is also pointing out this connection between Maundy Thursday and Good Friday, when he tells us:
For as often as you shall eat this bread and drink this chalice, you shall show the death of the Lord until He come (see Chapter 1).

Therefore, the Last Supper on Maundy Thursday and the Crucifixion on Good Friday, though separated in time, together form the one great act of our Redemption.

That is why, at the Consecration of the Mass, the priest also offers up to God, in Our Lord's name, what has become the Body and Blood of Jesus, in the same way as Jesus once offered the Sacrifice of His body and blood to His Heavenly Father on the cross two thousand years ago.

In other words: just as it was the body and blood of Jesus that He offered up once on the cross to His Heavenly Father to make up for our sins, so, at every Mass, Jesus continues to offer Himself to His Heavenly Father, for us, through His priests, under the form of simple bread and wine.

The Blessed Sacrament then, is at the heart of the Mass and of the Faith. Jesus ordained it to be the continuation throughout generations, and right across the world, through the priests of His Church, of His one great offering on Calvary. Each Mass is offered by Jesus to the Father for the living and the dead, in other words for us all.

In the prayer, 'The Morning Offering', we say:

> O Jesus, through the most pure heart of Mary, I offer Thee all the prayers, works, sufferings and joys of this day, for all the intentions of Thy Divine Heart in the Holy Mass.

This means that we are uniting ourselves with every Mass that is taking place across the whole world that day, even if we are unable to go to Mass ourselves. What a really wonderful thought that is!

As the words of consecration are pronounced, the host the priest holds up, all the other hosts he intends to consecrate on the altar, and the wine in the chalice become Jesus Himself, just as it was Jesus Himself on the cross.

The consecrated hosts, not received in Holy Communion during Mass, are then put into the Tabernacle after Mass. The sanctuary light is left on to show that He is there. That is why we genuflect when we go into a Catholic church, because Jesus is there really present.

This is the meaning of the term 'The Real Presence'.

Plate 11: A Tabernacle

If, for some reason the sanctuary light has been turned off, this may mean that the Sacrament is not reserved there at that time, and so of course we do not need to genuflect. Usually you will find that the light is on.

Jesus gave this precious gift of being able to 'consecrate' to His apostles at the Last Supper, so that they in turn could pass this on. Future priests would then give Our Lord Jesus in Holy Communion to all those, like us, who were to be born in a later time, until time itself will come to an end.

This is the teaching of the Catholic Church. We believe it because Our Lord told us, and His word is true. He told the apostles and disciples who walked with Him. This is what they believed. The apostles, disciples and all the early Christian martyrs believed this. They, themselves, died horrible deaths rather than deny the teachings of Our Lord. This is what every Pope and Council of the Church has taught, constantly, from the time of Jesus.

This way, both by Tradition, which is the passing down through the generations, and through Holy Scripture, the Blessed Sacrament, which is at the heart of the Faith, is passed down to us.

Chapter 9

THE MASS: SACRAMENT AND SACRIFICE

Thousands of years before Jesus came, the devout Jewish people would offer sacrifice to God in praise, thanksgiving and love. To make a sacrifice means to part with something you really very much want to keep, out of love for the person for whom you make the sacrifice.

The ancient people, out of love and out of reverence for God, would sacrifice the very best of their animals to Him. Animals were very important to them. They made their living by rearing cattle and swapping their animals for other things, which somebody else needed, in return for something they needed and did not have. So it 'hurt' them to part with the most precious ram or bull they had. As an offering to God, they would build a fire, kill the beast and burn it completely to ashes, so the smoke went up towards heaven.

Plate 12: Noah making a Sacrifice

Those were the sacrifices of the Old Testament, foreshadowing the New. Jesus, if you remember, brought the New Pasch. The greatest sacrifice that anyone can offer is the sacrifice of their life. Pleading for our sins, He, the Second person of the Blessed Trinity, offered to God His Father and ours, His body, blood, soul and divinity on the cross.

You know that the Blessed Sacrament is a sacrament. As well as a sacrament, however, it is also the supreme, perfect and unique sacrifice. That is why we talk about 'The Sacrifice of the Mass'.

Now that we have this perfect sacrifice of Jesus, there is no need for anyone to burn animals. But in our small way each one of us can make our own small sacrifices to add to the perfect sacrifice of Jesus. We can offer our lives up to God. We can do without things we want, just to please Him. This is why grown ups, as well as making a special effort to read holy books in Lent and Advent, do without sweets and the treats they have at other times. To sacrifice something we want means to do without it, as an offering of love.

Remember that little prayer, the Morning Offering, where we offer up to God everything in our day, the day that God gave us. We offer up not only our joys, but also the little things which have hurt us.

Chapter 10

WELCOMING JESUS

Our Lord gave us this wonderful miracle, because He loves us so much that He wants to remain with his Church always until the end of the world. He wants to feed, and to abide, which means to stay, to remain with all of us, with every man, woman and child for whom He died.

If a very special friend comes to visit us, what do we do? We try our best to make them feel as welcome as possible. We do all we can to show our love. Perhaps we tidy up the room where we are going to talk to them. Perhaps we put a vase of fresh flowers on the table. In the same way, we should prepare our hearts and minds to receive Jesus and make an Act of Contrition to say that we are sorry for our sins.

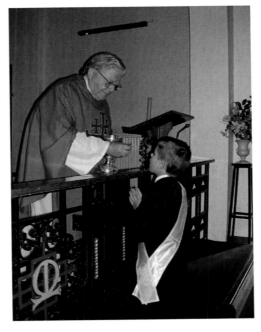

Plate 13: First Holy Communion

This way, when Jesus comes into our hearts (our 'room'!) everything will be clean and tidy and beautiful for Him. So when He arrives all we need to do is to talk to Him and have the tremendous joy of just having Him with us.

Of course, we must be very devout every time we receive Our Lord. We should walk up quietly praying and also ask Our Lady to help us to make a good Holy Communion.

All of us, grown-ups too, have to try to concentrate on talking to Him for as long as possible after we receive Him. We were told as children that Our Lord is with us particularly closely for a quarter of an hour. This has to do, I think, with the time it might take to digest the host we receive. This may not be considered entirely accurate today, but it still makes sense to concentrate very hard on Our Lord for at least this long and not to rush straight out of church and chatter to other people.

It is easier not to be distracted if we keep our eyes shut or keep our hands in front of our eyes. We can say we love Him, thank Him for all the good things in our life, especially for Holy Communion. We can pray for all those we love, for our friends and family who have died, and all those whom we know to be ill or unhappy for whatever reason. We can ask Him for all we feel we need.

Of course we should say sorry to him for any small sins we may have committed since our last Confession. Holy Communion has the power to forgive these sins.

We can also tell Jesus of all our worries, fears and hopes. Of course He will know these already as He is God, but He still likes us to tell Him and to ask Him for help.

Remember, you can tell Jesus anything, even things you feel you could not tell anyone else. Try also to listen to anything He may want you to understand.

Jesus is the greatest and truest friend you will ever have.

Chapter 11

ST. JOHN TELLS US MORE

St John was known as 'The beloved disciple' of Jesus. He was present at the most important moments of Jesus' public life on earth and followed Him everywhere. At first, he, like the others, was frightened by the soldiers and ran away when Jesus was arrested. He soon returned to Jesus, though, and was the only one to stand at the cross beside Our Lord with Our Lady, His mother.

St John lived to a great age after most of the other disciples had died or had travelled far away. Members of the Christian community, that is the early Church, went to him hoping for long sermons about Jesus. All he would say, when he was very old, to grown ups and children alike, was 'Little children - love one another'. This was how he summed up all of the teachings of Our Blessed Lord. St John wrote the last of the four Gospels, and so is one of the four 'Evangelists'. The other evangelists are St Matthew, St Mark and St Luke.

Plate 14: St John the Evangelist

In his Gospel, St John tells us that Jesus, teaching in the synagogue in Capharnaum, said:

47. Amen, Amen I say unto you: He that believeth in me hath everlasting life.
48. I am the bread of life.
49. Your fathers did eat manna in the desert and they died.
50. This is the bread descending down from heaven, that if any one eat of it, he may not die.
51. I am the living bread, which came down from heaven.
52. If any man eat of this bread, he shall live for ever: and the bread which I will give, is my flesh for the life of the world.

Then we are told:

53. The Jews therefore, debated amongst themselves, saying: How can this man give us his flesh to eat?
54 Then Jesus said 'Amen Amen I say unto you: Unless you eat the flesh of the Son of man and drink his blood, you shall not have life in you.
55. He that eateth my flesh and drinketh my blood, hath everlasting life: and I will raise him up at the last day.
56. For my flesh is meat indeed and my blood is drink indeed.
57. He that eateth my flesh, and drinketh my blood abideth in me and I in him'   (John vi: 47-57)

Some people found these words very shocking and went away, because they just didn't want to hear any more. St John's Gospel goes on to tell us:

67. After this, many of his disciples went back and walked no more with him.
68. Then Jesus said unto the twelve (to the twelve apostles). 'Will ye also go away?' Then Simon Peter anwered Him, 'Lord, to whom shall we go? Thou hast the words of eternal life (John vi: 67-69).

Notice Peter's reaction: there was nobody else they could go to, because only Jesus could give us eternal life. In the Gospel verses given above, Jesus explained that the only way to have eternal life was to eat His flesh and drink His blood. Because they knew Jesus so well, his apostles trusted Him, leaving Him to explain, in His own time, what He had meant by these strange words.

In a way one can hardly blame the people who on hearing this walked away from Him. Not only was Our Lord making extraordinary claims, but the whole idea sounded shocking. Certainly nobody else had ever suggested giving their body and blood to other people as their food and drink. It is not really a very nice thought, is it?

The point here, of course, is that they had no idea of the beautiful and homely way in which Jesus, God the Son, was to make this extraordinary thing happen.

How could they imagine that Jesus would give His very self, entirely, body, blood, soul and divinity in the simple form of bread made by human hands, and wine from the grapes that we grow?

Chapter 12

JESUS 'THE GOOD SHEPHERD'
AND ' THE SACRED HEART'

Our Lord founded the Church on Simon Peter. He was the first Pope. Simon Peter loved Jesus so much that he said he would die with Him. He really meant these words but, in his human fear of the soldiers, he denied Our Lord three times.

Plate 15: St Peter

In the Gospel of St Luke, (Luke xxii: 33-34), we read:

And he said to Him 'Lord I am ready to go with thee to prison and to death. And He said: 'I say to thee, Peter, the cock shall not crow this day till thou thrice deny that thou knowest me'.

Thrice means three times.

When Jesus had been arrested, they led Him, bound, to the High Priest's house. Peter, afraid, huddled by the open fire in the courtyard, hoping nobody would notice him. But a woman recognised him and said he was one of Jesus' followers.

57. But he denied Him, saying: 'Woman, I know Him not.'
58. And after a little while, another seeing him said: Thou also art one of them. But Peter said: O man, I am not.
59. Another man affirmed saying: 'Surely this man was also with him: for he is also a Galilean.
60. And Peter said: 'Man, I know not what thou sayest.' And immediately the cock crew.
61. And the Lord, turning, looked at Peter. And Peter remembered the word of the Lord, how He had said: 'Before the cock crow, thou shalt deny me thrice.'
62. And Peter went out and wept bitterly (Luke xxii: 57-62).

Poor Peter, how terrible he must have felt! He, who really loved Jesus, now remembered what Our Lord had said.   How weak had been his love when it was put to the test!

Holy people down the ages have had visions of the life of Jesus, seeing details not recorded in the Gospel, so we cannot be sure that they are true, but their comments are often very interesting. Such people are known as the 'mystical writers'. One of these says that the look Jesus gave Peter was only a quick glance, as he did not want the soldiers to see it and arrest Peter. But that glance of love and sadness from Our Lord, at such a time, must have broken Peter's heart with sorrow!

This story helps us, though, to realise that even Peter, the first Pope, was a human being like us, lacking courage, like we so often do when we are afraid to do the right thing.

Jesus wanted to give Simon Peter strength, so he changed his name from Simon to 'Cephas' or 'Peter', which means 'rock', because a rock is something very strong.

After His resurrection from the dead, Jesus asked Peter three times if he loved him more than the rest. He asked Peter the same question three times, because Peter had denied Him three times. The first time Peter answered

'Yes Lord', Jesus forgave him and said 'feed my sheep'; the second time Peter said 'Yes Lord', Our Lord said, 'feed my lambs' and the third time Peter answered 'Yes Lord, thou knowest all things, thou knowest that I love thee,' Jesus repeated, 'feed my sheep'.

Plate 17: The Good Shepherd

We are his sheep and his lambs, and so are all his followers from one end of the earth to the other, and from the beginning of time until the end of the world.

Before His Passion, knowing He would shortly be leaving them, Jesus had also said something very touching. He said:

I will not leave you orphaned; I am coming to you (John xiv: 18).

He was, of course, true to His word. He sent His own Holy Spirit down to the Apostles at the first Pentecost; and at the Last Supper He had already given His very Self to all His 'little ones', which means us too, throughout the ages in Holy Communion.

Like for Confession, we think of Jesus as 'the Good Shepherd' when thinking of Holy Communion. But equally important is another of Jesus' titles, that of 'the Sacred Heart'. We have many pictures and statues of Our Lord, which show a picture of a tiny heart on His chest.

This is because human beings, from ancient times, have always thought of the heart as the centre of emotions, especially that of love. This is not in fact medically true, as our emotions come from our brain. But the idea remains with us even today, doesn't it? Think of St Valentine's Day cards, and people who have 'I ♥ my mini' on the back of cars.

We have that little picture of a heart before our eyes, in order to keep before our minds how deep, true and abiding, is the great love of Jesus for each one of us.

Plate 17: The Sacred Heart

Could you imagine a better way of being really close to all people of all time than this great self-gift of Jesus? As his open arms, on the cross, embraced the world, so through the Eucharist Jesus lovingly stretches out His hands to each one of us personally. I hope you will grasp that hand and hold it all the days of your life.

There is a hymn by Jane Leeson, which goes:

> Loving Shepherd of thy sheep,
> Keep me Lord in safety keep;
> Nothing can thy power withstand,
> None can pluck me from thy hand.

The power of Jesus is stronger than any other.

Do you remember me singing to all of you when you were little the French song 'Entre les Etoiles', which is French for 'Up among the stars'? You will each have a copy of this and one day may learn to understand the French. That little song shows how each one of us has our special place in God's sight, where He lives in Heaven. He planned for us even before our birth, watches over our life, and waits for us to come home to Him when we die.

Learn about the person of Jesus through the Gospels and prayer books, especially during Lent. He was not a gushing, sentimental person, who just *said* 'I love you, I love you'. He proved it. Remember: 'A greater love no man hath than He lay down his life for his friends'. We are His friends.

He did yet more. Because He is God, He is able to continue this offering of Himself, His Body and His Blood in the Blessed Sacrament, through time, so that He can abide in each one of us, and we can each of us abide in Him. He wants us to be 'one' with Him as He is 'one' with the Father.

Try to use the sacraments Our Lord gave us, to keep close to Him, and to live in His light. Then, when you die, you will go straight to Him.

Remember that 'God made us to know Him, love Him and serve Him in this world and to be happy with Him forever in the next'.

The Blessed Sacrament has been in the Church ever since Our Lord was on earth, and will remain there until the end of the world. Our great, great, great grandfathers and grandmothers will have received Our Lord in their day.

The Faith is a tremendous gift.   If you keep it and pass it on, which it is your very solemn duty to Our Lord to do, then your great, great grandchildren may also receive Him in their day, long after you are dead.

Isn't that a fantastic thought?

THE BACKGROUND TO
THE BLESSED SACRAMENT

You now know most of what you need to know in order to receive Our Blessed Lord for the first time. But there is also some interesting background in the Old Testament of the Bible, which you might like to read about now or perhaps when you are older.

Chapter 13

LONG BEFORE JESUS CAME ON EARTH

To lead up to the institution of this Sacrament of love by Jesus, we need to go back to long before His time: God, as you know, created the world out of nothing by His word alone. He said 'Let there be light' and there was!

When we make something we make it from something else, which is already there. That is the difference between the word 'make' and the word 'create'. Only God can create.

In the first book of the Old Testament, called Genesis, we learn important parts of our Faith through a story about the first man and woman, our first parents, created by God, whom we call Adam and Eve. They lived with God in some wonderful place or in some wonderful 'way', which we call 'Paradise'. They had God's friendship, and were blessed by Him with many gifts, which we no longer have.

But God had a law, and Adam and Eve broke it. They disobeyed God. That was the first recorded sin of disobedience by mankind. It is called 'Original Sin' and every human baby born into the world inherits this sin. This is why little babies must be baptised, and grown-ups too sometimes, to take away what is often called 'the stain' of this sin, and also to make them members of the Church of Jesus Christ.

Jesus, who, as God, was sinless without the need to be baptised, was Himself baptised by St John the Baptist. He did this as an example to us, and to comply with the Jewish law. In His words:

> Amen, Amen I say to thee, unless a man be born again with water and the Holy Ghost, he cannot enter the Kingdom of Heaven (John iii: 5).

Plate 18: The Expulsion of Adam and Eve from the Garden of Eden

God is not mocked. God was offended. Our first parents whom we call Adam and Eve were disgraced and punished. They suddenly found themselves alone on this earth with nothing to protect them. There were no houses, no tools even to build a shelter, and no shops for food or clothing. They had lost all the special gifts, which God had given them. From then on, they and all their descendents, which means their children, their children's children and so on, had to work very hard to survive hunger, thirst, cold, and the threat from wild animals. They were now able to feel pain. They had to work very hard just to stay alive.

The very worst thing of all was that they had lost the precious friendship of Almighty God and had now lost the chance to go to Heaven and live in God's love for all eternity. Eternity means forever - without beginning and without end. It is something hard to imagine, isn't it? We are so used to 'time': lunchtime, teatime etc.

Mankind had somehow to make up to God for this sin. This is just like when you have been naughty, you need to be forgiven and make it up with your parents, and return to their friendship and love. Unfortunately, though, no sinful man alone would ever be able to make enough amends to Almighty God.

Only God Himself could therefore solve this problem.

> **For God so loved the world as to give His only begotten Son; that whosoever believeth in Him may not perish but may have life everlasting. For God sent not His Son into the world to condemn the world; but that the world through Him might be saved** (John iii: 16).

These beautiful words were also set to music called 'The Crucifixion' by the composer J. Stainer; one day you might sing it.

Chapter 14

NOAH, ABRAHAM AND THE PROPHETS

God promised a Saviour, to save us, but Jesus did not come for thousands of years. God spoke to the really good people like Noah. In fact God told Noah to build his ark and fill it with every beast and bird, and then sent a great flood and made a fresh start with Noah and his family, who were devout and obeyed God.

Another really good person was Abraham, and God promised Abraham that from his descendents, which means from his sons and grandsons, down the generations, the Saviour would be born. Jesus was in fact a direct descendent of Abraham.

Plate 19: The Departure of Abraham

There were also the prophets. These were holy people, who spoke in God's name. One of the greatest of these prophets was Moses, the Law Giver, to whom God gave the Ten Commandments. Some other well known prophets leading up to the birth of Jesus are Isaiah, Jeremiah, Ezekiel, Daniel, Amos, Mica, Malachi and the last of the prophets was St John the Baptist.

Throughout the Old Testament, prophets, like Isaiah, whom I mentioned before, came and spoke of the coming of the Messiah. This is another word for Jesus meaning 'anointed one', whom the Jews had so long awaited. They thought he would come to deliver them from being governed by the Roman Empire. They were wrong, because Jesus really came to save all generations from sin and not to settle arguments or injustice in any particular time in history.

The prophets 'foretold', which means 'said in advance', some exact details of the birth, teachings, death and resurrection of Jesus, many hundreds of years before these things happened. That is why we say that Jesus 'fulfilled' the prophecies.

Chapter 15

JESUS COMES ON EARTH

As you know, Jesus, who is God, also took our own human nature and became man. That is what the word 'Incarnation' means. Through the power of the Holy Spirit of God, Jesus was born of the Virgin Mary, like you were born from Mummy, and came to us as a tiny baby that first Christmas in the middle of the night.

Plate 20: The Baby Jesus

He is God and also is man. He has a human nature as well as His Divine nature. As man, when on earth, He knew fear, pain, hunger and thirst, just like us and grew up with all the problems we have. He taught us how to live. To the Jews of His time, He confirmed the Old Law of the Ten

Commandments, which God gave to Moses, and summarised them very simply:

You must love the Lord your God with your whole heart, mind, soul, and strength and your neighbour as yourself for God's sake (Mark xii: 30).

When asked who our 'neighbour' is, Jesus told the parable of the Good Samaritan, I am sure you will have heard of this.

Our Lord founded the Catholic Church on His apostles, with Peter at their head, in order to continue, through all generations to come, His work on earth. Finally, He did what He came on earth to do: He suffered a terrible death on the cross, offering all His sufferings to make up to God for all the actual sins of the human race, and also for that first 'original sin' of Adam and Eve, which had stopped everyone who was born after them from going to Heaven after death.

Chapter 16

TYPES OF CHRIST AND OF THE EUCHARIST

The Jews for generations learned about what we call the 'types'. 'Types' of Christ and 'types' of the Eucharist, meaning really similar things, lesser things that foreshadowed what was to come, things that were leading up to the big events.

Types of Christ:

Venerable John Henry Newman, whose story you can read in my next book, wrote a hymn called 'Praise to the Holiest in the Height'. There is a line that goes:

A second Adam to the fight and to the rescue came.

This 'second Adam' is Christ, Our Lord. Adam is known as a 'Type' of Christ. Adam and Eve, our first parents, disobeyed God. Jesus, Son of God, 'atoned', which means made up for Adam's sin. 'Atoned' means that Jesus made us 'at one' again with the Father, from whom sin had separated us. By the great sacrifice of His life, which was for all of us, we were able to return to God's friendship.

The Jewish Feast of the Passover, on which Our Lord, who was a Jew, chose to institute the Blessed Sacrament, itself commemorated a great event in Jewish history. This was the passing, about thirteen hundred years before, of the avenging angel over all the houses, sparing only those which had the blood of the Lamb smeared on the door posts, to show that the Feast of the Pascal Lamb had been observed in that home according to the command of God.

That Pascal Lamb was also a 'type' of Christ, which is why we speak to Jesus calling Him 'Agnus Dei' or 'Lamb of God' in the Mass.

Plate 21: The Lamb of God

The sun is another 'type' of Jesus. At Benediction we are blessed with the consecrated Host contained in the centre of a monstrance, which is a golden vessel like a blazing sun. When Jesus comes again to judge the world, He will come from the East, where the sun rises. This is why Catholic churches, where possible, face the East to greet the Risen Lord.

Types of the Eucharist:

As told in the Old Testament and also shown in St John's Gospel, given in Part One, when the Israelites, travelling in the desert, had no food, God let 'manna' fall from heaven to feed them. They just had to pick it up. It seems to have been a soft, white bread-like substance, which kept them fed happily. This manna was a 'type' or fore-shadowing of the Eucharist, the real Bread of Heaven which, generations later, Jesus was to give us.

Our Lord was reminding people in St John's Gospel of that manna, which God gave the Israelites long, long before his time. He told us that manna was just ordinary food, whereas the consecrated bread would give 'eternal life.'

Another 'type' of the Eucharist is the feeding of the Five Thousand and of the Four Thousand. You will have read about these occasions by now, I am sure. Our Lord said then, when people were so amazed how a bit of bread and a few fishes could miraculously feed so many people, that the real Bread of Heaven was yet to come.

Jesus, Himself a Jew, and His apostles, also Jews, converted large numbers of Jews to the 'New Pasch'. Jesus told His followers to carry to the ends of the earth all that He had commanded of them, the fullness of the Catholic, which means universal, Christian Faith.

But some Jews remained, who did not accept that Jesus was the Messiah. The Jews throughout the world today are the descendents of those who could not believe that Jesus was He, whom God had promised to send for our salvation, to save us from sin and Hell.   In the Bible,   they are called Israelites.

As Jews are a race of people, a person of the Jewish race converting to Catholicism remains a Jew, only a Catholic one.   The French Cardinal Lustiger, who died in August 2007, aged eighty, was himself a Jewish convert.

Plate 22: Cardinal Lustiger

As I said at the beginning, this is really more than you need to know now, but I hope you will come back to it when you are older and can understand more. Then I hope that you will want to read about these fascinating things yourself in far more detail than the brief sketch I have given you here.

Chapter 17

THE TWO FEAST DAYS
FOR THE BLESSED EUCHARIST

<u>First Feast - Maundy Thursday</u>

The first feast is, of course, Maundy Thursday itself, when Jesus instituted it at the Last Supper the day before He died. Because He was a Jew, descended from Abraham, if you remember, He wanted to eat the Pasch or the Jewish Pascal Feast with His friends for the last time, and to use this setting to institute the New Pasch, which is the Blessed Sacrament or Eucharist.

On Maundy Thursday, during the singing of the Gloria in the Mass, bells are rung. Then there is complete silence until Easter is ushered in by Holy Saturday. The altar is stripped of all cloth. The Blessed Sacrament is taken in procession to the altar of repose, in the Monstrance, after which there is adoration before the Blessed Sacrament through most or all of the night.

Plate 23: The Monstrance held up by Bishop Rifan

As the priest and servers process to the Altar of Repose, the most beautiful hymn, 'Pange Lingua', is sung in churches all over the world. It is usually sung in Latin, which I think is more poetic than the English translation, so I hope that one day you may learn some Latin.

You may need to read this ancient poetry several times to understand it but, when you do, I think you will learn to love it. Part of this is the 'Tantum Ergo' which is sung at Benediction.

Whenever you can, try to go to Benediction. At the Brompton Oratory, in London, especially on the Feast of the Sacred Heart, (held on the second Friday after the Thursday of Corpus Christi) it is particularly beautiful.

Benediction is a wonderful homage, paying respect to the Most Blessed Sacrament. We are literally 'blessed' by the Blessed Sacrament in the monstrance, mentioned above, where you can see Jesus in the white consecrated Host in the centre. When the Blessed Sacrament is exposed like that, we need to go on both knees rather than just one, when coming in and going out of church.

Early Christians complained that they could never 'see' the Blessed Sacrament, over the heads of other people. This is one of the times that the Church listened to the voice of the people ('vox populi' in Latin). When the priest held up the monstrance high, and held it out to right and to left, in blessing, then everybody could see Jesus Himself in the Blessed Sacrament, and bow down in adoration.

<u>Second Feast - Corpus Christi</u>

It was not until the year 1264 that the great Feast of Corpus Christi, in thanksgiving for the Blessed Sacrament, was given to the Church by Pope Urban 4th, to be celebrated on the Thursday after Trinity Sunday.

Maundy Thursday was the actual day that Jesus instituted the Sacrament, but other things on that day, such as the Washing of the Feet of the Apostles by Our Lord, fill much of the liturgy in the Mass on that day. The word 'liturgy' means the Church's public Prayer.

So, Catholics across the world, prompted by the prayers of a holy nun, Juliana, from Liège, which is now in Belgium, asked for a special Holy Day, just to commemorate the great Sacrament of Sacraments - another occasion of 'vox populi'.

Plate 24: Corpus Christi Procession in Campos, Brazil

You will read under 'Stories' that St Thomas Aquinas and St Bonaventure were both asked by the next Pope, Gregory 10th, to write a special 'Sequence', which is the part just before the Gospel, for this new Mass of Corpus Christi. They were both very famous theologians living at that time. A theologian is somebody who makes a study of God.   It comes from the word 'Theos', which means God in Greek.

When I was at school this long Sequence would sometimes, of course, be sung right through in plainchant, like the Mass you sing at your local church, the chapel at Wardour Castle.   It could also be divided up into sections, which were sung polyphonically on different occasions. Polyphonic singing means several people singing the same words to different tunes, which all blend together harmoniously.

St Thomas' Sequence, the 'Lauda Sion', was chosen.   Other parts of the 'Lauda Sion', which we used to sing separately, are the 'In Hac Mensa' and the 'Caro Cibus', which were set to music by Mendelssohn and specially arranged for us to sing at my school, Farnborough Hill, by our head of Music, Dr Wardale.

The 'Ecce Panis' is usually sung to 'an old Portuguese melody' and the 'Bone Pastor', which means Good Shepherd, was set to music by Miguel Eslava amongst others. Even without music, the words themselves have a rhythmic quality, which is prayerful.

You may remember that Grandpop and I brought the French Catholic academic association C.I.E.L ('Centre International d'Etudes Liturgiques') to England. People with high academic qualifications would give talks every year all about the liturgy, or public worship, of the Church. I remember at one CIEL UK conference, the main speaker decided to end his talk with a flourish and quote, in Latin, the end of the 'Lauda Sion', the 'Bone Pastor'. He was surprised that once he had started, the Conference Chairman, Lord Gill, and others joined in with him with great enthusiasm, as they all knew it off by heart. So it was an even more dramatic end of a speech than the speaker, Professor John Saward, had intended!

I hope you will read the 'Lauda Sion' one day and see how the rhythm carries you through it.   The words and the sense are also beautiful.

The 'O Sacrum Convivium' is another well known Latin hymn about the Eucharist.

Also, it is on the Feast of Corpus Christi that we have that beautiful Epistle from St Paul to the Corinthians (1 Corinthians xi: 23) quoted in Part One, where St Paul passes down to us what had been passed to him, about how Jesus consecrated bread and wine into His own Body and Blood; into His very self.

The Fall of mankind from the Grace of God, made a 'Saviour' necessary to reunite man to God . That is why Jesus came. But as well as redeeming us and restoring us to God's love, He taught us how to live in God's grace on this earth. Most importantly of all, by instituting the Blessed Sacrament, He made sure that His 'sheep' of all generations would be able to know, love Him and be united with Him, through the Holy Spirit, as He and the Father are 'one'.

What a wonderful thing that every one of us has the chance of Holy Communion with Jesus, just like the apostles did over two thousand years ago! When you grow up, if you have children of your own, you can tell them also all about this treasure, which will lead them to heaven.

Remember Our Lord's words:

Seek ye first the kingdom of heaven and all else will be added to you.

Plate 25: Our Lady - Queen of Heaven

PRAYERS AND HYMNS

EVERYDAY PRAYERS

Our Father, who art in Heaven,
Hallowed be Thy name,
Thy Kingdom come,
Thy will be done
On earth as it is in Heaven.
Give us this day our daily bread, and
Forgive us our trespasses
As we forgive those who trespass against us
And lead us not into temptation,
But deliver us from evil.   Amen

Hail, Mary, full of Grace,
The Lord is with thee:
Blessed art thou amongst women,
And blessed is the fruit of thy womb Jesus.
Holy Mary Mother of God,
Pray for us sinners now,
And at the hour of our death.   Amen

Glory be to the Father,
And to the Son,
And to the Holy Ghost.
As it was in the beginning,
Is now, and ever shall be,
World without end. Amen

Hail, Holy Queen, Mother of Mercy;
Hail our life, our sweetness and our hope.
To thee do we cry,
Poor banished children of Eve.
To thee do we send up our sighs,
Mourning and weeping in this vale of tears.
Turn then, most gracious Advocate,
Thine eyes of mercy towards us.
And after this our exile,
Show unto us the blessed fruit
Of thy womb, Jesus.
O Clement, O loving O sweet Virgin Mary.
Pray for us, O holy mother of God,
That we may be made worthy of the
Promises of Christ.   Amen

I believe in God,
The Father Almighty,
Creator of Heaven and earth.
I believe in Jesus Christ
His Only Son Our Lord,
He was conceived by the power
Of the Holy Spirit
And born of the Virgin Mary.
He suffered under Pontius Pilate,
Was crucified, died and was buried.
He descended to the dead.
On the third day He rose again.

He ascended to Heaven
And is seated at the right hand
Of the Father;
He will come again
To judge the living and the dead.
I believe in the Holy Spirit;
The Holy Catholic Church;
The Communion of Saints;
The forgiveness of sins;
The resurrection of the body,
And life everlasting. Amen

Child's Daily Prayer

Gentle Jesus, meek and mild,
Look on me, a little child.
Pity mine, and pity me.
Suffer me to come to Thee.
Heart of Jesus, I adore Thee;
Heart of Mary, I implore Thee;
Heart of Joseph, pure and just:
In these three hearts I put my trust.
Amen

Plate 26: Child Praying

Prayer from Cecily's school

O God our Father,
I have come to say
Thank you for your love today.
Thank you for my family and
All the friends you give to me.
Guard me in the dark of night
And in the morning send your Light.
Amen

Armistice Day Poem

Remember, remember,
who died, in November,
May they rest in silence
May they rest in Divine waters,
May the rainbow cover their hearts
Remember, remember,
who died in November
                        by Cecily Perry Robinson
                                aged 7 years

Prayers for Confession

Eternal Father, I thank you for the grace of this Confession.
My Jesus, how good and kind you are!
You have washed away my sins with your precious Blood.
O Holy Spirit, you have given me light to know my sins.
I beg the light of your grace.
I beg this so that I may go
And never sin again. Amen.

Plate 27: Children Kneeling in Prayer

Prayer before Holy Communion

Jesus Christ, I want You
Jesus Christ, I want You
I want You for my own sake,

Because I am so weak,
Because I am a sinner,
Because I am nothing.

I want you for Your sake,
So that I may know You,
So that I may love You,
So that I may become like You.

I want You for the sake of others,
So that I may never harm them,
So that I may always do good to
                    them,
So that I may give You to them.

Jesus Christ, You want me -
You want me for Your own sake,
Because You made me,
Because You died for me,
Because You love me.

You want me for Your sake,
That I may be Your joy,
That I may be Your crown,
That I may be one with You.

You want me for the sake of others -
That through me You may heal others,
That through me You may teach others,
That through me You may come to
them.

Jesus Christ, You shall have me -
All that I have,
All that I am,
All that I possibly can be. Amen

Act of Love and Desire

Sweet Jesus, I love You.
I desire with all my heart
to receive You.
Most sweet Jesus,
Come into my soul

And give me Your Flesh to eat
And Your Blood to drink.
Give me Your whole Self;
Body, Blood, Soul and Divinity,
That I may live forever with You.
                    Amen.

Morning Offering

O Jesus, through The most pure heart of Mary,
We offer you all the prayers, works, sufferings and joys of this day
For all the intentions of Thy Divine Heart In the Holy Mass. Amen

Act of Offering

O Jesus, receive my poor offering.
Jesus, You have given Yourself to me, and
Now, let me give myself to You:

I give You my body, that it may be chaste and pure.
I give You my soul, that it may be free from sin.
I give You my heart, that it may always love You.
I give You every breath that I shall breathe,
and especially my last;
I give You myself in life and in death
That I may be Yours for ever and ever.

Sweet Jesus, I am going away for a time,
but I trust not without You.
You are with me by Your grace.
I will never leave You by mortal sin.
I do not fear to do so, though I am weak,
because I have such hope in You.
Give me grace to persevere. Amen

Plate 28: Jesus as a Child

Prayers after Holy Communion

Act of Faith:
O Jesus, I believe that I have received
Your Flesh to eat and Your Blood to drink,
because You have said it,
and Your Word is true.

Act of Adoration:
O Jesus, my God, my Creator,
I adore You, because from Your Hands I
came, and with You I am to be happy forever.

Act of Humility:
O Jesus, I am not worthy to receive You,
And yet You have come to me that
My poor heart may learn from You
To be meek and humble.

Act of Love:
Sweet Jesus, I love You;
I love You with all my heart.
You know that I love You, and
wish to love You daily more and more.

Act of Thanksgiving:
My good Jesus, I thank You
with all my heart. How good,
how kind You are to me, Sweet Jesus!
Blessed be Jesus
in the Most Holy Sacrament of the Altar.

Prayer for Help

You love me Lord, and I love You.
You are calling me and I am ready.
You invite me to Your heavenly feast.
The Food You give me is Your Holy Body.
You give this Food that I may live forever.
You are the Resurrection and the Life.

Jesus, Great God! Jesus, Good Shepherd!
I want to be with You always.
My Lord, I believe in You; I love You.
Give me Your Light.
Give me Your Strength
Give me Your Holy Spirit
Come into my soul and stay forever.
Your Will, not mine, be done.
My God, teach me.
Help me to help others.

I love You.
I hope in You.
I trust You and leave all to You.
I am sorry for my sins.
I thank You.
I praise You.
I ask You for all I need.
I long for You now.

Dear Lord, Thank You for coming to me.
Stay with me and make me always
Yours. With Your help I can be good.
Make me loving and kind to everybody.
Let me see You in everyone I meet.
Bless especially those I know who
Are dear to me, and bring to Heaven
The souls of those who have died.
Help me to work hard at school,
especially with my homework.
Dear Lord, thank You for coming to me.
Let me stay close to You always. Amen

Grandy and Grandad's - my parents - Favourite Hymn

Lord for tomorrow and its needs
I do not pray;
Keep me, My God, from stain of
sin,
Just for today.

Let me most diligently work
And duly pray;
Let me be kind in word and deed,
Just for today.

Let me be slow to do my will
Prompt to obey;
Help me to mortify my flesh
Just for today.

Let me no wrong or idle word
Unthinking say;
Set thou a seal upon my lips
Just for today.

And if today my tide of life
Should ebb away,
Give me thy sacraments divine
Sweet Lord today.

So, for tomorrow and its needs
I do not pray;
But keep me, guide me, love me,
Lord
Just for today.

Child's Night Prayer

Jesus tender Shepherd hear me
Bless thy little lamb tonight,
Through the darkness be Thou near me
Keep me safe till morning light.
All this day thine hand has led me
And I thank thee for thy care
Thou hast warmed me, clothed and fed me
Listen to my evening prayer.

Let my sins be all forgiven
Bless the friends I love so well
Take me when I die to Heaven
Happy there with Thee to dwell.
Amen

Maggie Sherwood's Prayer
learned from her mother, Ida Knapton

Chapter 18

'JUST STORIES'

The stories in this book start with quite simple ones, with accounts of a few famous saints from the early Church. There is also a brief sketch of early Roman martyrs and saints after whom my grandchildren are named.

After reading one or two chapters from the first part of the book, these stories are just meant as some extra reading for fun.

ST ANTHONY AND GRANNY AND GRANDPOP

This is a short and very strange story. To this day, I cannot say what really happened, so you see what you think. The story of St Anthony of Padua is later in this section, but you will all know that he is the saint we pray to for help, if we have lost something important.

It was the night before Grandy's birthday, 24th October, 1950, and I was nine years old. Grandy had already shouted up the stairs that she was coming up to tuck me in any minute.

But I had not yet wrapped up her birthday present for the next day! I was really worried that she might come up and catch me in the middle of wrapping up her present and the whole surprise would be lost.

I had bought for her a lime green and white mottled pottery jug, which I had thought very pretty, but feel sure now from memory that it was in rather poor taste. Certainly I do not remember her ever using it.

All my life, when wrapping presents, I have found it hard to keep track of present, paper, scissors and sellotape. I am always losing one of them. Having made a start, I heard Grandy again shout up to say she was just coming.

I suddenly mislaid the sellotape. Panic set in. WHERE was it? I looked under the bed, under the chairs, rushed all round the room and it was nowhere to be seen. Grandy could be coming up any minute and find the parcel half wrapped. At that age, this moment was one of crisis.

I went on my knees and with a burst of real fervour cried out "PLEASE St Anthony!!"

Plate 29: St Anthony of Padua

A second after my prayer, the sellotape rolled, diagonally from the door, straight into my hands.

By the age of nine, we had been taught at school not to rush to the idea of miracles, because there is a perfectly natural explanation for most things. Also, I could not see why St Anthony should have considered favouring me with a miracle on such a trivial matter. But at the time it was a very serious matter to me, and I had prayed with great intensity and total faith.

Could that sellotape have gone on rolling round throughout all that time I had spent looking under the bed and the chairs? It could well have done I suppose. Also, I had possibly taken less time doing this than I thought.

But if it had been rolling round, why had it come 'straight' from the door? And that is what I remember. But then I am thinking back fifty-eight years, and it is hard to be sure.

Some years ago, I asked my friend Father Straub what he thought about this. He said he thought it perfectly possible for St Anthony to grant a miracle to a young child, who called out for his help with such trust.

Well, I don't know. What do you think?

St Anthony has helped me all my life. Many years later, when your parents were grown up, Grandpop had lost Grandma's camera, only a short while after her death. He was very upset at losing her camera, and we searched everywhere, particularly in the car and the boot as we were on holiday.

I prayed to St Anthony. When we still had not found it I asked Grandpop if he himself had prayed to St Anthony. He had not, so I suggested he did, as it was his camera. He then asked St Anthony for his help. The next time we looked into the car boot there was the camera in quite an obvious place.

Of course we might not have looked thoroughly enough before, but I feel personally sure St Anthony guided our searching when we went to him for help.

ST PADRE PIO AND GRANNY

St Padre Pio is a very modern saint, canonized on 16th June 2002. He was still alive when your own parents, Dominic and Amanda, were little children. You will find out all about him under 'Stories' in the next book.

Padre Pio is very important to me and I say a novena prayer to him each day. A 'novena' comes from the Latin word 'nine'. It is usually only said for nine days. Of course you can say it every day if you wish. The one I say is called 'The efficacious Novena of Padre Pio'. The word 'efficacious' means that it works!

Plate 30: St Padre Pio

Many years ago now, the daughter of an old friend of mine gave birth to twins. They were beautiful babies. But, it was soon discovered that the little boy had a serious disease called 'Cystic Fibrosis'.

He had it so badly that the doctors did not think he would live more than a few weeks. Because the baby boy had this illness, they tested the little girl, who seemed perfectly well, just in case. Very sadly the tests showed the little girl also had it. This disease can affect either the lungs or the digestion, or both. The doctors said that both the twins had it 'severely' in both areas.

The worst part of the disease is that on top of being very often ill and having to have nasty treatments, those who have it never live much beyond twenty and very many die much earlier.

Before he was ten days old, the baby boy had had three major operations to help him to breathe and to digest his milk. He was not expected to live as long as a year. But he was still alive at the age of two and by this time had had ten operations.

He was still likely to die any time and never expected to grow old enough to go to school. When they were born, I prayed to Padre Pio and put the lives of both these little babies into his hands. I have prayed for them every day of their lives since. I am still asking for Padre Pio's help for them after more than a quarter of a century.

They are now 26 years old! They are both very bright and have travelled to Australia, to America more than once, and to other interesting places across the world.

The little girl is now a beautiful young woman, who is a very good actress and has been in some well known films, and has been allowed into private rooms at film premiers, whilst most people are crowding in the streets.

That baby boy, considered a hopeless case, is now a young man, who has been able to go cycling in France to help raise money for the treatment of Cystic Fibrosis. He has been skydiving, which means being dropped out of an airplane and free-falling before opening the parachute. He has also done paragliding. They both ski well and have been white water rafting. So they have done many exciting things that other people, without their illness, would love to do and perhaps never will.

Despite missing between one third and half of his schooling, through being ill so often, the young man is very clever and won many awards as he grew up. He went to York University and last summer he heard that he had not only obtained 2.1 degree, which is an excellent degree, but also a special commendation for having managed to do this despite all the difficulties caused by this disease. He is at the moment in hospital and in need of your prayers.

Against ALL odds, Padre Pio has looked after these children every day of their lives. He must have looked after the boy particularly, as he was the smallest and weakest baby with this illness that their hospital had ever known.

Instead of dying before he was a year old, which all the doctors were sure that he would, he has now lived as long as young adults sometimes do, who have this disease, and much longer than others. Padre Pio has also looked after their mother, whose life has of course been very hard, and given her the strength to keep these delicate children safe and to help them to enjoy life to the full.

I believe that it is all due to the care of Padre Pio. During his lifetime God allowed him to work many miracles, and it seems that he continues to listen to those who ask him for help now that he is in heaven. So, if you hear of somebody in great need of help, you could always ask Padre Pio to join his prayers to God with yours.

THE STORY OF A RECENT MIRACLE
AT THE RUE DU BAC

This miracle took place in the late 1990s. The doctors had told the mother of a little girl that her daughter had a disease, which could not be cured. They had declared her case hopeless. Her daughter would soon die from the illness.

The family lived very far away in Brazil, where Bishop Rifan comes from. The mother and her little daughter travelled to France especially to pray in the various holy places where Our Lady had appeared.

They started their visit in Paris and went to the rue du Bac chapel, where Our Lady had appeared to Saint Catherine Labouré in the 19th century, showing to her the miraculous medal bearing the inscription:

O Mary conceived without sin pray for us who have recourse to thee.

The Blessed Virgin told St Catherine that she would shower graces upon those who implored her.

Plate 31: St Catherine Laboure

The mother told her little daughter the beautiful story of Our Lady appearing to St Catherine. She explained that the custom for pilgrims was to pray, touching the very chair upon which Our Lady had sat when she had appeared to St Catherine. The mother told her little girl to do this and to beg Our Lady to cure her.

Once in the chapel, they prayed together for a little while at the altar rails. Then the mother quietly told her daughter to go through the altar rails and touch the chair. Her daughter went up to the chair, but at the last moment stopped and simply knelt at the foot of the chair, very prayerfully, with her head to one side.

After a few moments she returned slowly to her place behind the altar rails and, shortly after, she and her mother left the chapel. Her mother was very disappointed that her daughter had not touched the chair, as she had told her to do.

They travelled around France and gradually the little girl's health seemed to be getting better. In fact soon she seemed to be quite well again. So they returned to Brazil to see the consultant doctor who had discovered her incurable illness. Medical tests no longer showed any trace of her disease!

The consultant begged the mother to tell him what they had done to bring about this extraordinary cure, so that he could try to help other children with the same disease.

The mother simply said that she had taken her child to the rue du Bac. The doctor, who was a Catholic, then said:

"But you say she did not touch the chair."

Then the little girl, sensing herself to be criticised, said for the first time:

"But the lady told me not to bother to touch the chair but just to rest my head on her knee."

This was the story, as I remember it, when it was told to me some years ago by David Smith, my friend in Paris, whose daughter, Marguerite-Marie, is Amanda's Godchild.

THE PILGRIM TEDDY BEAR

Some years ago now, a little boy called Anthony Readings, from our church at Chesham Bois, went on the Chartres Pilgrimage. You will learn all about the Chartres Pilgrimage in the next 'story'. When he came home he found he had left his teddy bear in France.   He had named his teddy 'Edmund Campion', after the Reformation Jesuit. You can read about him in Book Three.

Anthony was very upset as you can imagine, as he could not remember exactly where he had left him.

My friend, David Smith, who lives in France, organises the children's part of the pilgrimage. David managed to find the teddy and gave it to a friend, who was coming to England. This friend was able to pass it on to me, and I gave it back to Anthony. Maureen Readings, Anthony's mother, sent me photos of Anthony's delight at the return of Edmund Campion. You will see him in the picture with his Teddy Bear.

Plate 32: The Return of Edmund Campion

Of course Anthony is a big boy now. Last year in church, he spoke from the reading desk, to remind people that the year 2008 is the one hundred and fiftieth anniversary of when Our Lady of Lourdes appeared to the country girl, Bernadette Soubiroux. Anthony was encouraging people, especially teenagers, to come on the pilgrimage in this very special year.

THE CHARTRES PILGRIMAGE

The Chartres Pilgrimage is at Whitsun every year. Do try to go when you are old enough. It is a wonderful event, which gathers young people from countries all over the world. Quite old people do also go and struggle to complete it each year. Pilgrims walk for three days, the ancient seventy-two mile pilgrim route between the Cathedral of Notre Dame in Paris and the Cathedral of Chartres.

You have to really want to go in for this. You walk twenty miles a day, carrying your pack, sheltering in rather damp tents for the two nights. It usually rains at some stage and most people end up with sore, blistered feet. Happily, there are special plasters you can buy to protect feet to some extent against blisters these days. But the journey is a challenge, and is hard to complete. That is what a pilgrimage is really about: it is something hard you try to do for God. It was never meant to be easy.

It is actually much easier these days than it was centuries ago, because most of your luggage is taken for you to the campsites, so you only carry a very light pack. Also, water is given to you as you go along. Anyone who feels they can't walk any more is given a lift, although most young people try to walk the full way.

Plate 33: Our Lady of Walsingham

All along the route you sing hymns. Every different country has its own procession and carries its own banner. The British pilgrimage to Chartres was set up by Mrs Mary Carey from our congregation at Chesham Bois.

Her son, Francis, runs it now. Our national banner is that of Our Lady of Walsingham. There is Mass every evening and confessions on the way. People talk of a strange and wonderful feeling of the unity and timelessness of the Church.

Then, as for the pilgrims of the middle ages, there comes that great moment: the spires of Chartres Cathedral come into sight on the brow of a hill. Then, as they did hundreds of years ago, thousands of pilgrims fall to their knees in joy and sing the 'Salve Regina' in thanksgiving.

It is still a long way to the Cathedral, but the end is in sight, and the lucky ones are able to crowd inside the cathedral for a glorious Pontifical High Mass. The French are very hospitable and remain outside the cathedral so those from other countries may go in.

WAITING TO SEE THE POPE

There is a well-known story, but I cannot be sure if it is true, about St Thomas and St Bonaventure. They were two famous theologians living at the same time and their stories are told later in this the book.

St Thomas and St Bonaventure had both been asked by Pope Gregory 10th to write a 'Sequence' to form part of the 'Proper' of the Mass for the new feast of Corpus Christi.   The Sequence comes just before the Gospel.

They were both waiting to be shown in to the Pope, and give him the results of their work, so the Pope could choose between them. Before going in, St Thomas and St Bonaventure swapped over the poetic prayers, which they had composed. Each read each other's contribution.

As soon as he had read through St Thomas' 'Sequence', St Bonaventure immediately tore his own work up, as he could appreciate the far superior quality of St Thomas' prayer, which is called the 'Lauda Sion'. (See the story of St Thomas Aquinas later in this section.)

THE STORY OF A PRIEST

This is a story about the priesthood.   When you get married, you only promise to remain together until 'death do us part'. Priests, who are ordained by bishops, become priests 'in aeternum', which is Latin for forever. This means that you continue to have this special priestly nature in your soul even after you are dead. So it is far more serious if a priest decides he wants to break the sacred vows, or promises, he made before God always to be a priest.

Sometimes, though, there are good reasons why a priest may be released from his vows.

Over the last forty years there has been much unrest in the Church. This has resulted in many more priests than usual across the world seeking to be released from their sacred vows. Pope John Paul II realized this, and he needed a very good reason to allow a priest to become 'laicised'. That means to become an ordinary member of the laity like us, and no longer to be a priest.

One such priest asked his bishop if he could be released. Permission was denied. He felt so strongly about this that he travelled to Rome to see the last Pope, Pope John Paul II. He managed to get a personal interview with the Pope, which is always a very hard thing to do, as Popes are very busy.

When he went before Pope John Paul, he explained to him exactly why he was an exception and really needed to be released from his vows to be a priest. Pope John Paul listened carefully to his reasons. He gave permission for the priest to be released from his vows. However, the Pope had one condition:

He said: 'But first, please will you hear my Confession', and knelt down before the priest. The priest was so overcome by this request that it made him weep. Then the Pope explained to him how wonderful a gift it was to be able, through the power of the Church, to forgive sins, even the sins of a Pope who, like us, is human and has need of God's forgiveness.

Plate 34: Pope John Paul II

The priest was so moved by this that he no longer wished to be laicized.   He walked out of the room resolving not only to remain a priest, bringing Jesus to the hearts of people, but that he would be the best possible priest he could be.

Chapter 19

EARLY CHRISTIAN MARTYR STORIES

Grandchildren's Saint Names

The word 'martyr' means 'witness'. A person who dies for the Faith is a martyr, but to be called a martyr he or she has to die for God. As St Augustine says: " Not the pain but the cause, or the reason why they die, makes the martyr".

Had it not been for the amazing Faith and zeal of the first Christians, the Church founded by Our Lord Jesus would not have taken root. That it did so was because the Holy Spirit gave those early witnesses the courage they needed to face unimaginable terror, pain and death.

St Stephen was the first Christian martyr, who was stoned to death whilst he stretched out his arms in prayer and gazed up towards heaven. Many Christian martyrs were killed by fire or the sword or else fed to the lions for sport in the huge Roman Coliseum.

Since some of my grandchildren have the names of early Christian martyrs, I would like to paint a short word picture about each of them.

St Cecilia, Virgin and Martyr - Feast Day November 22

Plate 35: St Cecilia

Cecilia, or Cecily, is one of the most famous of Roman martyrs. Tradition has it that she lived and was martyred when Urban 1st was Pope during the third century. It was not until the sixth century that she became really venerated, or honoured as a Saint.

It all happened a long time ago, so it is hard to be certain of the details of the early Christian martyrs, especially of the life of St Cecilia, as there is confusion between her and a later Cecilia.

We have to rely on what we have from the tradition and legends of the early Church. According to these, Cecily, a Christian, was born of a noble family, and was engaged to a man called Valerius.

As she had already vowed her virginity to God, she did not wish to marry him, as her vow meant that she could not be a proper wife to Valerius. Cecily converted both Valerius, and also his brother Tiburtius. When the rulers of Rome discovered they had become Christian, they were both arrested and martyred.

After she had buried their bodies, Cecily was herself brought before the Prefect of Rome. She refused to worship a pagan god, and even managed to convert her persecutors.

The Christian faith had too many enemies at that time, so she still was sentenced to death. The plan was to suffocate her in her bathroom. The heat and steam failed to kill her, so a soldier was sent to behead her. Three blows failed to kill her, but she died three days later of her wounds.

Pope Urban the First then dedicated her house as a church. He had encouraged her to stand by her vow to God. The church in her honour is in Trastevere and is one of the oldest in Rome. When her remains were discovered in the year 822, they were laid to rest here. One day you might like to visit this church.

Cecily became the patron saint of music in the 16th century. The reason given for this is that, according to tradition, as the organs played during her wedding feast, Cecily sung in her heart to the Lord, saying: "may my heart remain unsullied (pure), so that I be not confounded" (overcome).

An account of her life is famous as the 'Second Nun's Tale' in Chaucer's *Canterbury Tales*.

Cecilia is the patron of Albi Cathedral and various English churches and convents. Her main emblem is the organ, but it is sometimes the lute. There are cycles of her life in stained glass windows at Bourges, dating from the 13th century. There are also 15th century frescoes, which are ancient paintings on the wall, at the Carmine church in Florence.

St Cecily or Cecilia is named in the Canon of the Mass. Our Cecily was born thirteen days before the Feast day of St Cecilia.

St Agnes, Virgin and Martyr - Feast Day January 21

Plate 36: Dedication of St Agnes to Jesus forsaking all worldly temptations.

Together with St Cecilia, St Agnes is one of the most famous and well-loved Roman martyrs. We hear about her as early as the year 354.

At the height of persecution, when many of the faithful, and even the priests, were to afraid to stand up for the Faith, she remained faithful to Jesus and made the sacrifice of her young life. Early Fathers of the Church, St Ambrose, St Damasus, St Jerome and St Prudentius, all praised the example that she gave.

When she was only twelve or thirteen, Agnes refused marriage, like St Cecilia, because of her dedication to Christ. Calmly she preferred death to breaking her vow. The early Church venerated her because of her great courage. Tradition tells us that she left her home and offered herself for martyrdom. She was killed by a sword, which pierced her throat.

Because her name 'Agnes' was so like the word 'Agnus', or lamb, her emblem is a lamb. At the church San Apolinare Nuovo at Ravenna, there are 6th century mosaics showing this.

On her Feast day special lambs are blessed. Their fleeces are used to make pallia for archbishops. A pallium is a kind of shawl that is given to archbishops. Every year, the nuns of St Agnes' convent in Rome weave the wool from the lambs to make these shawls.

At the beginning of the fourth century, when peace was restored to the Church, there is clear evidence that the princess Constantina, the eldest daughter of Constantine, the first Christian Emperor, built a basilica (church) over her tomb. There is little doubt that the remains of St Agnes are indeed in this tomb. This is one of the most ancient and famous tombs in Rome. You could visit it when you go to Rome.

In England, there were five early churches dedicated to her, and there are also many shrines and villages with her name that we have ourselves visited in Cornwall and Wales.

The finest part of her life story is on a gold and enamel cup at the British Museum. It used to belong to the Duke of Berry, and passed through the Duke of Bedford to King Henry VI.

Like St Cecilia, St Agnes' name is in the Canon of the Mass.

St Sebastian, Martyr - Feast Day January 20

Plate 37: St Sebastian's Martyrdom

St Sebastian shares a feast day with St Fabian, Pope, as these two saints have always been venerated together. Their names were always together in the ancient books about martyrs. They are also together in the Litany of the Saints. I have read that they remained together in the Roman Canon of the Mass in early times. If so, perhaps that was a very long time ago, because although Fabian is included in the oldest missal I have, Sebastian is not.

Again, since he is such an early saint, one has to rely on tradition and legend for details of his life and martyrdom. According to these, Sebastian was a Roman soldier who enlisted in 283 in Rome. From the ruins of the Roman Forum, my friend, Merryn Howell, and I looked up at the woods in the hills, where he would have been garrisoned. There is a photo of her pointing to them.

Sebastian, who was a Christian, helped the faith of fellow Christians, Mark and Marcellian, by visiting them in prison. Diocletian, the most vicious persecutor of all the Roman Emperors, and the last to persecute Christians, did not know that Sebastian was a Christian. He promoted Sebastian to the rank of Captain.

When Diocletian discovered that Sebastian had supported other martyrs, he accused him of ingratitude and ordered him to be shot to death by arrows.

Although he was shot full of arrows, he was not quite dead. According to legend, a kind lady found him, took him home and nursed him back to health. Then, when he had fully recovered, he bravely returned to Diocletian and confronted him with his cruelty.

Perhaps Sebastian thought he could save his soul. But Diocletian knew no mercy and ordered him to be beaten to death, this time with clubs.

Sebastian is the patron saint of archers. His feast day is the 20th January, two days before the birth of our Sebastian.

The well-known Basilica erected in honour of Sebastian is in the Appian Way in Rome.

A much later Saint
Saint Elisabeth Rose - Feast Day December 14
Abbess of Rosoy-le-Vieil around 1130

Plate 38: St Elisabeth Rose founded an Abbey in Rozoy-le-Vieil

Since my third granddaughter is called Elisabeth Rose, here is a little story about the life of this saint.

About as little is known about Saint Elisabeth Rose, as is known for sure about the Roman Martyrs, despite the fact that she lived much later. There are big gaps in her life and, sadly, the Proper for her Feast has been lost. It may only have been used around the area where she lived.

She was christened Elisabeth, possibly after the mother of St John the Baptist, as the more famous saints by that name, such as Elisabeth of Hungary and of

Portugal were after her time. She was Parisian, born into a noble, in fact royal, family. Her parents were called Rodolphe and Adèle.

When she grew up she spent some years at a monastery at Chelles. One day, when it was her turn to read the lesson in the refectory, she asked the Mother Abbess to allow her to leave the convent. She asked permission to be a hermit and live in the wild with only snakes and lizards for company.

Elisabeth set out with two companions towards Gâtinais. They had to travel right through the then huge forest, which is now called Fontainebleau. They arrived at a castle, and the owner of this castle suggested she retire to nearby Rozoy.

Towards the end of the eleventh century and the beginning of the twelfth, hermits were very common. The land around Rozoy was perfect for that kind of life, with its thick woodlands and lakes. A hermit has a completely solitary life with nobody to talk to, so that they can fix their minds entirely on God.

What was unusual was that hermits were usually men, who decided to live such a hard and lonely life. The two nuns who went with Elisabeth were horrified at this wild country and so very soon went back to the monastery. Elisabeth, however, settled herself in the hollow of a huge oak tree, and lived in it as if it were a kind of nest.

This unusual oak tree was already well known by the local country people, or peasants. They had always thought of it with some superstition. When Elisabeth started living in the tree, the peasants from all round the area brought her bread, meat, fruit, butter and milk.

Elisabeth ate this food gratefully and gave anything over to the poor. Her behaviour was amazing: a young girl living alone in a swamp. She never went to church for Mass, to receive the sacraments or to recite the Divine Office, as she was living as a hermit. This was not what normally happened in the Church.

The peasants were not at all bothered about this and honoured this extraordinary young girl as if she were a saint.

As far as the Church authorities were concerned, it was hard to know whether to burn incense in her honour or to burn her. It was common in those days to burn at the stake those suspected of being witches, like St Joan of Arc.

They simply could not decide whether her behaviour came from God or not. Whilst they were still undecided, they took away her holy water, which was the one material thing linking her to the life of the Church!

It was terribly cold spending the winter in the hollow of an oak tree. Elisabeth had to mend her one dress so often that, in the end, it was more mending than dress. Despite all this hardship, she never thought for a moment of leaving her rough home.

However, when two other nuns came to join her, one of them being her sister, she had to agree to live somewhere a little more comfortable.

The local country people again came to her help. The men built a wooden hut for them, whilst their wives brought them food. Then later they even built a small chapel.

Elisabeth's fame spread and legend tells us that she brought about miracles using the waters in the local streams. To this day, in August pilgrims visit the local fountain which is said to be good for eye diseases and for the fertility of cattle and of women.

Elisabeth died around 1130. The monastery was quite well known in the twelfth century, but was later destroyed by the English. The nuns got together again in their Priory at Villechasson, which was only a few miles away from Rozoy.

'Elisabeth, Founder of the Monastery of Rozoy'

is all that is written, in Latin, in the Abbey of Paraclet. This simple mention probably dated from a time when she had not yet been honoured by the Church, and we still do not know when the 'Office' for her Mass was composed or by whom.

At some stage Elisabeth was given the name that was given to the monastery she had founded, the name Elisabeth Rose. This seems to be because the stream, which ran through Rozoy, sprung from a huge lake called Saint Rose, and the fountain of St Rose. Maybe it was the water from this stream which she used for her miracles.

So her name, Elisabeth Rose, was her baptismal name linked, some years later, to the place Rozoy, where she was a hermit. The word 'Rozoy' is likely to have derived from the lake of St Rose.

The most important document about this saint remains in manuscript form at the Bibliothèque Nationale and reads as follows:

> The story of the Abbey of Rosey, of the Order of St Benedict, in the diocese of Sens, gives the life of Elisabeth, first Abbess and founder of this religious house. Authentic records about this history are given by Fr Jacques Vignier S.J. in 1640.

Elisabeth Rose's Feast Day is kept on 14th December, six days before the birth of our Elisabeth Rose.

Saints Perpetua and Felicity - Feast Day March 7

Plate 39: St Felicity and St Perpetua

Our fifth grandchild is called Felicity. The stories of Felicity and Perpetua are so closely linked together, as you will see, that one cannot talk of one without the other.

Perpetua was the daughter of a rich nobleman of Carthage, which is now in Tunisia in North Africa. He was a pagan, which meant he did not believe in God. Felicity, who had known suffering already, as she had been a slave, was given the job of looking after the needs of Perpetua. The girls soon became close friends. They were about the same age, both recently married, and both expecting babies.

What united them more, though, was that they were both catechumens. That means that they were full of Christian faith, and were waiting to be baptized, when they had learned all that the Church taught about Jesus.

They both lived during the times when Christians, especially those who were waiting to be baptized Christians, were persecuted for their religion and often killed for it. The emperor at that time was Septimus Severus. I think we can be sure that he was 'severe'!

Perpetua's father did all he possibly could to persuade her to drop this Christian faith, from bullying her to pleading with her, but neither she nor Felicity would be put off their precious Faith. If necessary they would die for Jesus.

When it became known that they were Christians, they were both arrested, together with three young men who were also catechumens. But before they were taken into prison, they were all baptized, so that their faith could not be doubted by anyone.

Much more is known about these early martyrs than about most, because Perpetua and Saturus, one of the young men, wrote down the wonderful visions they both had, and gave details leading right up to their deaths.

By the time they were imprisoned, Perpetua had already had her baby boy, but Felicity was still only eight months' pregnant.

Felicity was very afraid that she might not be killed at the same time as her friends, because the law forbade the execution of pregnant women. So, she might have to go later, possibly not with fellow Christians but with thieves and murderers.

Perpetua was terribly worried about the little boy she had just given birth to, as she was breast-feeding him. The prison was horrible: they had been put in a part of it which was dark and damp, and the girls were very unhappy.

Two deacons were able to persuade those in charge of the prison to move the girls to a nicer part of it with more light and air. Also they brought Perpetua's baby boy to her. He was faint with hunger but soon recovered, now that she could feed him. She was allowed to keep him with her. Perpetua was overjoyed at this and described the prison now as a 'palace'.

At their trial, the six imprisoned Christians all stuck firmly to their belief in Jesus. Perpetua's father, holding her baby in his arms, begged her for the last time to give up this Christianity and save her life. He was driven away with a whip. The Christians were then condemned to be torn to pieces by wild animals in the amphitheatre, which is like the Coliseum in Rome. This would happen soon, during the 'Games', on the birthday of the Emperor Geta.

Two of these Christians were given wonderful dreams about their approaching martyrdom, which helped them to face it with joy rather than fear.

Felicity, if you remember, was afraid that the she might not be allowed to shed her innocent blood with her friends, as she was with child. The other Christians, wishing her to go to her death with them, all prayed so loudly to the Lord, that Felicity would give birth before the Games. This grace was granted to her, she had her baby early, just three days before the Games. Her baby girl was later adopted by a sister.

On the day before the Games it was usual, as it also was in quite modern times, for those to be executed the next day to have a last Feast the evening before they died. They chose to make this an 'Agape' or Christian Love Feast. The Adjutant of the prison and others by now also believed.

Before being led out, Felicity and Perpetua were told that they must put on the robes of the pagan priests. But they argued that the reason they were going freely to their death is that they would have nothing to do with pagan gods. So they were allowed to keep their own clothes. When they were led out to the amphitheatre for their martyrdom, the men went first and Felicity and Perpetua held hands, with their heads held high, smiling joyously as if going to heaven and not to be mauled by wild beasts. Felicity had only just had a baby, with little time to recover, so it must have been very difficult for her to stride so bravely in.

When they saw Hilarian, who had been their judge, the men said: "You have judged us now, but you also will be judged".

The people were so angry on hearing this, that they asked that they should be whipped by the gladiators, who would later fight with the beasts, before the animals were let out. They were all happy to share in this way the sufferings of Jesus.

When it was the turn of the two girls, a mad cow was sent into the arena to attack them. After the cow had mauled them, they were to be killed by the sword in the sight of all the people sitting round the amphitheatre.

The two girls gave each other the final kiss of peace, as a last witness to their Faith, before being beheaded.

They are known to be the bravest and happiest of martyrs. Early records show that they were honoured in Rome in the fourth century. That is why they are both in the Roman Canon of the Mass, although they both lived and died, in the year 203, in North Africa.

Their Feast Day is 7th March. Our Felicity was born on the Feast of St Felix and three days before the Feast of Saints Felicity and Perpetua.

Chapter 20

TWO SAINTS AUGUSTINE

SAINT AUGUSTINE OF HIPPO

Plate 40: St Augustine of Hippo

St Augustine was born in 354 and lived in Algeria, North Africa. His father was a pagan but his mother, Monica, was a Christian. She taught Augustine all about Jesus, although he was not baptized.

When he was sixteen, he went to school in Carthage. He was very clever. It was there that he met a woman he loved very much. He did not marry her but lived with her for fourteen years, which made Augustine's mother very unhappy. They had a son called Adeodatus (which is Latin for 'given by God').

When he had finished his studies, he started teaching. Augustine felt very unsettled. He was unhappy because he had not yet found a meaning to his life. He was very attracted by the ideas of Manichaeism, which was against Christianity. This heresy is explained in the story of St Anthony of Padua, as it flared up again a thousand years later!

Because he was so clever, he was invited to Italy, and was offered a job as a teacher in Milan. There, he met St Ambrose, who helped him to think about what God wanted him to do.

Augustine found it very hard to decide whether to continue his rich life of pleasure, which of course he was very much enjoying, or to give it all up, live a hard life and devote himself to God. He found it a very difficult choice.

Meanwhile, his mother, St Monica, never gave up praying for her son. She prayed that he would convert to the Christianity of his childhood. She knew that if he turned to God, he could do great things for the early Church. She was greatly consoled by the words of a bishop whom she had told of her distress: "It is not possible that the son of so many tears should be lost."

There is also the famous remark we are told that Augustine himself made: "O Lord, make me good, but not yet." How often do we all feel like this?

At last, Augustine's decision was taken in a garden when he read in the bible:

> The night is past, and the day is at hand. Let us therefore cast off the works of darkness and put on the armour of light.

> Let us walk honestly as in the day not in rioting and drunkenness, not in impurities, not in contention and envy, but put ye on the Lord JESUS CHRIST (Romans xiii: 12-14).

With his friend Alipius and his beloved son Adeodatus, Augustine was baptized on Easter eve in 387. He went back to Africa where he formed a monastic community. There he became a priest, and five years later was made Bishop of Hippo, in North Africa.

He went on living in his community. The Monastic Rule he set up has been taken over by other religious orders since, in particular the Canons Regular and the Canons of St Augustine named after him.

For the next thirty-four years he was a remarkable bishop. He was in the Sanctuary at Mass every morning, preaching every Sunday, baptizing his flock, attending to every possible pastoral duty as well as looking after the poor.

On top of this, he spent every spare moment in writing. Many of his books were fighting the great heresies of his day, but others were on the Trinity and Grace. He wrote a vast amount of books: 113 books, over 200 letters and 500 sermons, still survive today. It seems amazing that we should still have his work from the fourth century!

Two of his longest works are the 'Confessions', which give an account of his life up to the time of his conversion, and 'The City of God'. The second of these books was written at the time Rome was being captured by Alaric the Goth in 410.

The great Roman Empire was collapsing in the West. What did Augustine do? He quietly sat down and wrote another book!

He was on his deathbed, in 430, still writing when the Vandals were at the very gates of Hippo! That book, however, and Augustine's spirit have, like Catholic Christianity, survived many other empires as well.

Remember that Our Lord said to St Peter, on whom He founded the Church:

> To Thee will I give the keys of Heaven and the gates of Hell shall not prevail against it.

SAINT AUGUSTINE OF CANTERBURY

Plate 41: Pope Gregory (obscured) sends St Augustine to England

The second of the two famous Saints named Augustine is St Augustine of Canterbury, who was a Benedictine, and who was born about two hundred years after Saint Augustine of Hippo. Augustine of Canterbury is very important to us, because from early times he has been known as the 'evangelizer' of England, although not of Roman Briton.

Pope St Gregory the Great, in 596, sent him, with forty monks, to preach the Gospel to the heathen English. Heathens had not been taught about Christ and so, of course, were unable to believe in Him.

On a beautiful sunny day, Augustine and his followers arrived in Kent. The local king, King Ethelbert, was waiting to greet him, seated under a tree with his soldiers round him.

The first sight of Augustine, on the shores of England, was a long file of monks approaching from afar in procession. They carried a large silver cross at their head, and banners showing pictures of Christ. As they approached, their voices became louder singing Gregorian chant. According to Bossuet, the historian: "The history of the Church has nothing more beautiful."

King Ethelbert received them well, and became a Catholic with many of his subjects, which was hardly surprising after such a dramatic introduction to the Faith.

Augustine then went to Arles to be consecrated Archbishop of England. He established his See at Canterbury. A 'See' means a central place from which, as Archbishop, he could rule the local Church. There he also founded the Monastery of SS Peter and Paul. This was later renamed the Monastery of St Augustine.

It was a successful mission and Augustine founded two more Episcopal Sees, or places for bishops to rule, in London and in Rochester. He did not, sadly, manage to extend his mission to Wales and the South West of England, as these Britons were wary of him and would not be converted.

Augustine was not in England very long and did not cover much ground, but he achieved a great deal within his areas. We can read how hard he worked and what he did from the pages of 'The Venerable Bede', the great historian of those times. He gives us the replies sent by Pope Gregory to Augustine's many requests for direction and matters connected with his mission.

St Augustine of Canterbury died in 605.

Chapter 21

GREAT SAINTS OF THE MIDDLE AGES

ST THOMAS AQUINAS

Plate 42: St Thomas Aquinas

St Thomas Aquinas was born in 1225. He is generally thought to be the greatest Doctor of the Church. He was one of the many children of Landulph of Aquino, head of a large and noble family, near Lombardy in Italy.

Thomas went to a Benedictine school, at the famous Monastery of Monte Casino, and later he studied at the University of Naples. Whilst he was at Naples he decided to join the Dominican Order. The Dominicans were wandering Friars who preached God, in poverty, travelling from town to town.

The idea of this horrified his noble relatives and his brothers kidnapped him and shut him up for a whole year!

Thomas still would not change his mind. When he was released, he went to study at the University of Paris, and also in Cologne, which is in Germany. He was a large man of few words, so people called him 'the dumb ox'. He was really extremely clever, and shortly showed that his brain was as large as he was. He gained his degree as Master of Theology.

The word 'Theos' means God in Greek and theology is the study of God. Philosophy is the search for wisdom and knowledge, and the study of the ways of human thought which lead us to this knowledge. This in turn leads us to God. The Church owes much of her understanding of both theology and philosophy to the brilliant mind of St Thomas Aquinas.

Thomas spent most of his quite short life teaching, preaching and above all writing. He travelled around, whilst doing this between France, Germany and Italy, ending up again in Naples.

Despite his huge brain, he showed remarkable humility. That is why he is known as 'the Angelic Doctor'. He was a 'doctor' because of his 'doctorates' or university degrees. It was said of Brother Thomas that although he was a genius with a brilliant mind, he would never have done all the things he did had it not been for his great love of God and devout life of prayer.

As a true Dominican he handed on to others the fruits of his contemplation or deep thoughts.

Amongst his most famous writings are: *Summa contra Gentiles* and *Summa Theologica.* He left his great *Summa Theologica* unfinished in 1273. He said that it was but straw compared to all that he had seen and had revealed to him.

Summa contra Gentiles is about God and His creation in three large books, but the *Summa Theologica* runs to twenty-two volumes! This was a step-by-step explanation of theology of such depth that it gained him the title of 'Doctor Communis' or 'universal teacher'.

Thomas was called to the General Council at Lyons in France, but he was very ill and died on the way, in 1274.

Perhaps because of his very humility, he had less influence on the Church in his time than others such as St Bonaventure and St Albert. It was only after his death that his fame grew and his enormous contribution to the Church was realised.

In 1556 Pope Pius V declared him a Doctor of the Church, and in 1889 Pope Leo XIII, through an encyclical letter, which only a Pope can write, encouraged a great revival and renewed study of St Thomas's works and teachings in depth.

Thomas Aquinas also wrote many beautiful hymns, among the most famous being the *Adoro Te Devote*, 'O Godhead hid devoutly we adore Thee', *Verbum Supernum*, 'The word of God proceeding forth', the *Lauda Sion*, 'Sion, lift thy voice and sing', and 'Praise thy Saviour and thy King'.

The emblem of St Thomas Aquinas is a star.

Though St Thomas Aquinas was a high-powered, brilliant theologian, we must remember that he is a saint, not just for what he did, but for what he was. He lived a life of humble prayer and service, centred on Jesus Christ. Whether or not we are clever like he was, we can try to imitate his humility.

ST BONAVENTURE

St Bonaventure, born in 1221, was a deeply learned Franciscan friar, given his name by St Francis himself, who had cured him of a childhood illness. His real name was Giovanni di Fidanza. St Bonaventure left Italy to work for his doctorate in Paris, where he taught and preached for a number of years.

He was there at the same time as St Thomas Aquinas and together they defended the begging life of the friars against their many enemies. He was later head of the Franciscans and was thought to be the greatest Friar Minor after St Francis himself, almost like a second founder.

In 1265 he was offered the archbishopric of York, which he did not take up, but eight years later he became Cardinal bishop of Albano. He helped draw up the agenda for the Council of Lyons, taking a very important part in this until his death during this Council in 1274. He was canonized in 1482.

One of St Bonaventure's sayings is:

> No one can be happy unless he rise above himself, not by raising the body, but by raising the heart. But we cannot rise above ourselves unless a higher power lifts us up. A divine aid is always there for those who seek it from their hearts, humbly and devoutly.

Chapter 22

ST FRANCIS OF ASSISI

St Francis was born in 1182 in the almost magical hilltop town of Assisi in Italy. He died there in 1226 aged only forty-four. During his short lifetime he made a far greater impact on the spiritual lives of the people of his time than any other person had done before. He actually changed the history of the Church.

St Francis is known as the most radical Christian in two thousand years. That means that, like Jesus, he turned upside down the ideas of the people at the time when he lived. He cut back to the bare roots (which is what radical means) of Christianity: when all the people around him were striving after money and power, he chose to live humbly and in total poverty. He turned his back on the rich, comfortable life he had been born into, in order to live the Gospel to the full.

Plate 43: St Francis singing to the Birds

Our friend Dorothy Johnson, who went to Assisi before we did, described it as being 'placed between heaven and earth'. This was because there was a cloud covering the first part of the hill and the top rose above the clouds into deep blue sky looking like a fairy castle.

Francis' father was a wealthy cloth merchant named Pietro Bernardone and his mother Pica was French. He was christened Giovanni, but because he loved France so much, his father changed his name to Francesco, which means 'little Frenchman'. The family lived up the hill, where the rich people had their homes. All the rubbish and sewage went down the hill to the poor people, who lived at the bottom!

It was a romantic time and everyone sang songs about love, and also about the glories of being a soldier. Francis grew up in a pleasure-seeking world, with dreams of being a knight and one day falling in love with a beautiful woman.

As a teenager, he had plenty of money. He was a born leader, and spent most of his time partying with his friends. At the age of twenty, he took part in a minor battle between Assisi and the nearby town of Perugia. He was captured and sent to prison, where he became ill. His father paid for him to come home, but he was still ill for a long time. Then in 1205 Francis, full of warlike ideas, headed off again to be a soldier to fight the Germans. But he became ill again on the way and had to return home.

A change came over Francis when back home and he started wandering round visiting a broken-down church just outside Assisi named San Damiano. He was praying and a voice from the crucifix said:

> Rebuild my church, which as you see is falling into ruin.

This inspired Francis, and he began to live a life of penance. He sold some of his father's cloth to buy the stones he needed for the church.

His father was furious: not only had Francis not become the great soldier he had hoped he would, but he had poor health. He was already disappointed in him. That he had now sold his cloth to build a church was the last straw.

He asked his son for the money back but Francis refused, so the local bishop was called in to settle the matter. All the people in the town gathered outside to hear the outcome. The bishop sided with Francis' father, Pietro.

Then Francis made his dramatic gesture; he said:

> From now on it is not my father Pietro Bernardone, but my Father who art in Heaven.

On saying this he returned all his clothes to his father and would have walked out of the city naked, had the bishop not given him something to wrap around himself!

Plate 44: San Damiano Crucifix

Francis started to beg for stones. Although many of his old friends laughed at him, he continued slowly to rebuild San Damiano. When San Damiano was rebuilt, he moved on to rebuild another ruined church, Santa Maria degli Angeli. There, he heard a sermon on the 10th chapter of St Matthew, in which Jesus spoke to his disciples sending them into the world:

> Cure the sick, raise the dead, cleanse the lepers and cast out devils ... You received without charge, give without charge. Provide yourself with no silver, no spare tunic or footwear or staff, for the workman deserves his keep.

Francis knew that God was speaking to him and that, from then on, this would be his life. Now, he would be a knight for Christ and at last he had found his true bride: 'Lady poverty'. He had been given an old tunic by the Bishop of Assisi and wore no shoes.

Soon, he was joined by others in the town, including some of his once rich group of friends. When he had twelve followers, they went to Rome to obtain approval for his new Order. Pope Innocent III granted this request in 1210, to the scruffy-looking band, who based their lives on St Matthew's Gospel.

St Francis founded an order for women, headed by St Clare of Assisi. They called themselves the Poor Clares, and were also devoted to poverty, preaching Christ and caring for the sick .

Plate 45: St Clare of Assisi

Clare was believed to be a very beautiful girl who, like St Francis, saw the emptiness of seeking wealth above all things, and wanted also to choose holy poverty, to live the Gospel of Christ. St Francis gave her a worn tunic like his followers wore, and symbolically cut off her long beautiful hair.

St Francis arranged for Clare to live at first in a small convent, but her family were trying to bring her back home. The Bishop gave Clare the church of San Damiano and the house next to it. Soon she was joined by two of her family. They made their Franciscan vows and became part of the Order.

This was the Second Order of St Francis. It grew quickly and was known as the Poor Clares, or more officially the 'Order of St Clare'. But St Clare did not actually write the Rule for her Order until 1253, twenty-seven years after the death of St Francis.

St Francis also founded a Third Order of Franciscans, who wished to carry on a life within the world, but with the spiritual guidance of the Franciscan Rule. This was not a religious Order but a 'secular' one, which means one for people leading an otherwise normal life.

However, the First Order of Francis was that of the Friars Minor, and consisted of those who had first joined him living rough in the forest. The Franciscans travelled in pairs throughout Italy and then into Europe, preaching that the kingdom of God was close at hand.

There are many strange and miraculous stories connected with St Francis. Once he ordered one of his friars to go to nearby Arezzo to cast out devils, as there were wicked people living there. St Francis himself was seen levitating, which means rising above the ground, and also bilocating, which means being in two places at once.

It is hard here to separate truth from legend, because there are so many stories of this kind. But the number of such stories show how amazingly well known and admired he became in his short lifetime. People were so won over by the freshness of his simple Gospel teaching, that his three Orders gained 5,000 members in just a few years. Once, St Francis was even asked to preach to the Pope.

St Francis' thinking about war had completely changed; it was also now ahead of his time. He wanted to seek peace through talking rather than fighting. He made the enormous journey to Egypt to meet the Sultan Mali-al-Kamil in 1219, hoping to convert him to Catholicism.

Can you imagine this? A poor ragged Italian, bare foot, trudging across the world, and on his arrival asking to be shown in to the mighty Sultan in his sumptuous palace! Though the Sultan and St Francis respected each other and became friends, the Sultan would not change his religion. So Francis returned home. Although he had not won over the Sultan to Catholicism, his action made people think about seeking a peaceful solution to avoid the bloodshed of war.

St Francis loved nature and saw the reflection of God in everything. He talked to Brother Sun and Sister Moon. He even rejoiced in bad weather as it came from God. He preached to birds encouraging them to praise God by their flying and singing. He was the first person to rejoice in every part of the natural world, plants and animals, and to encourage us to treasure them as part of God's creation.

The most famous animal story was when he actually tamed a hungry and therefore dangerous wolf, which had been roaming round the town of Gubbio, and terrifying the people. It may be that the wolf was eating their animals on which they depended for food and attacked the owners when they tried to stop it.

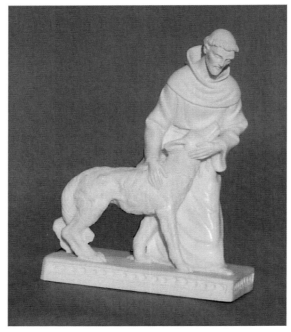

Plate 46: St Francis taming the Wolf

The story goes that St Francis went directly to the wolf, whom he greeted in the name of Christ! He made a pact with the wolf: the people in the town would leave food for the wolf and in return the wolf would leave them in peace. They then shook hands on it! St Francis offered his hand and the wolf gave him his paw. Brother Wolf became St Francis's friend and nobody was afraid of it anymore.

He saw Christ in all the nature around him and especially in poverty. Jesus, the king of the world, was born in a stable and died like a criminal on the cross. Francis wanted to follow the poverty of his divine Master as closely as he possibly could.

St Francis was never healthy and suffered from various illnesses, about which he never complained. One day, in 1224, whilst at prayer, he saw a six-winged angel bearing the five wounds of Jesus. He then received the 'Stigmata'. That means that St Francis himself was given the very wounds that Jesus had in his own hands, feet and side. This was the first ever case of the 'Stigmata'. The stigmata changed the skin on the soles of his feet into the shape of a nail, which stuck out. So as walking was too painful, he had to wear sandals. That is where the tradition of Franciscans wearing sandals comes from.

The pain of these wounds never left him and he also became severely ill. In 1226 in Assisi, half blind, he died of tuberculosis, welcoming Sister Death.

Tradition has it that one of his brothers, who had never been able to talk, and was also on the point of death in the south of Italy, shouted out "Wait for me Francis, I am coming with you."

There were many miraculous cures reported just after his death, and of a dying woman being brought back to life so she could confess a mortal sin.

The Pope was at one point uncertain about the truth of the Stigmata, but St Francis appeared to him in a dream, and filled a vial full of blood from the wound in his side. St Francis was so holy as to be allowed to do what he had most wanted to do: to suffer with Christ. After he died his Stigmata were studied and declared to be a scientific fact.

He was canonized only two years later, in 1228. His Feast Day is 4th October.

In 1978 his coffin was opened and was shown to contain the bones of a man around forty with tuberculosis of the spine.

Grandpop and I were very lucky to have been shown round Assisi by Michael and Maria-Cecilia Woolgar. My own son, Dominic, was at school with their son Dermot, and Amanda knew him too through the Order of Malta Volunteers, who look after the sick in Lourdes every summer.

It was wonderful to go with them around the Basilica di San Francesco. It stands out against the sky and is in the shape of a Tau cross. This is a cross in the shape of a T. In the days when St Francis lived, people went to great lengths to get hold of relics of saints, and St Francis was known as a saint in his lifetime. For this reason, his friars were very afraid that people might try to steal his body. So, when he died, they put his body in a tomb surrounded by stone slabs and metal bars. As early as 1228, only two years after his death, work was started to build a cathedral over the top of this tomb to protect it.

In 1997 there was an earthquake, which made the roof of the Upper Church crash down. Happily the all-important 28 frescoes, or wall paintings, by Giotto di Bondone, showing the stages of St Francis' life, can still be seen. The view of St Francis, that there was the fingerprint of God on every leaf and in the beauty of every animal, changed the attitude of his time towards art. Instead of just figures, and what they were doing, there came to be much more natural scenery to show the beauty created by God.

In the Lower Church is St Francis' tomb under the altar, which is known to be one of the holiest places in the world. One has this thrilling sense of spirituality when in the Lower Church, and we all genuflected before it.

The Woolgars were wonderful guides, and it was a privilege, which we will never forget, to be shown all the sacred places connected with St Francis by people who knew and loved it so well.

Try to find a book by Paul Gallico called 'The Small Miracle'. It is all about a little boy from Assisi who owns a donkey. The donkey becomes ill and the little boy is convinced that the only way he would be cured is by taking him to the tomb of St Francis. But the donkey cannot get down the steps, and the priests in charge of the church are not helpful to the little boy. It is a beautiful story about a child's faith and the continuing spirit of St Francis.

Attached to the Church there is a museum, where there is a large room filled by a very long table, containing in miniature, not only the nativity scene, but lots of other little scenes of workmen, women and children in caves. It shows what other people in Bethlehem were doing at the time of the birth of Jesus. As you move round the table, all the figures move. I hope one day you might have the chance to go to see this delightful work of art. It is all due to St Francis that we have the custom of the Christmas crib. He even acted out the Nativity in the town of Greccio with a real baby.

Plate 47: Nativity Scene

The Basilica of Santa Maria degli Angeli, the second church rebuilt by St Francis, was again rebuilt in 1927 after an earthquake had damaged the one there before. Inside it has a jewel! In the middle of the huge church is the tiny chapel that St Francis had built with his own hands. It is called the Portiuncula, which means the tiny patch of land surrounding the original church, on which St Francis built his chapel in the middle of a forest. One can kneel by it and touch the stones he placed there with his own hands. Just imagine you are in the original forest where the whole Franciscan movement began in this tiny chapel!

At the end of his life, Francis handed over the running of his Orders and withdrew from the world. He wrote his famous work, *The Canticle of Brother Sun*. Also, much can be learned of him from the book *Fioretti* or *Little Flowers of St Francis*.

He is the patron of Assisi, of the environment and of the blind.

I took the name of 'Francis' for my Confirmation, and Amanda has 'Frances' as her second name.

Not just amongst Catholics, but also amongst people of other Faiths and none, St Francis remains one of the best-loved saints of all time.

St Francis, Pray for us.

Chapter 23

ST ANTHONY OF PADUA

Plate 48: St Anthony of Padua

St Anthony of Padua, which is in Italy, was not Italian but Portuguese. He was born in Lisbon in 1199 and christened Ferdinand. His parents, like those of Saint Francis, were wealthy and had high ideas for their son. They wanted him to have an important job and add to the fortunes of the family. Again, like St Francis, Ferdinand wanted only to serve God and lead a humble life.

As young as thirteen he left home to join an Augustinian Abbey just outside Lisbon. He had a very fine mind and learned a great deal from the good Canons, who are rather like monks. The trouble was, he was still too close to home and people kept visiting him.

He asked his Superior to move him to another monastery further away in Coimbra, which was then the capital of Portugal. Even here, he felt life was just too easy and comfortable. He longed to follow the call of Christ to leave everything and follow Him.

It was at this monastery that he met five Franciscan Friars, who were on their way to Morocco in Africa, to try, as St Francis himself did, to preach the Gospel to the Muslims, rather than to fight them. Ferdinand wished he too could go on such a mission. The Muslims killed the good Friars, who were martyred for their Faith. Rather than putting Ferdinand off, he wanted all the more to go to Morocco and try to convert souls for Christ.

The Head of the Augustinian Order allowed Ferdinand to join the Franciscan Order. In 1220 he was given the rough clothes that the followers of St Francis wore. He learned about the teachings of St Francis. In this new life he took the name of Anthony.

He then went to Morocco with another friar. But when he arrived, he caught malaria and became so ill that he could not walk. He was forced to leave Africa and return home. But more trouble was in store for him. The boat was driven off course by a terrible storm and landed in Sicily, which is the island just below Italy. Here he met some more friars and joined them.

Whilst he was in Sicily, there was a world 'Chapter' of the Franciscans. This meant that all the followers of St Francis, working across the world, were called back to Assisi, in Italy, to renew their spiritual lives. There were now thousands of Franciscans, and this great gathering was known as the 'Chapter of the Mats', because there were not enough beds for the friars, who mostly had to sleep on mats!

St Francis, by this time, was too ill to give a homily to this huge mass of people, so he whispered what he wanted to say to a fellow friar who preached aloud for him. St Anthony actually heard the preaching of St Francis, but there is no record of them ever having met and spoken.

After the Chapter was over the friars all returned to their friaries, and Anthony was sent to a small mountain community of hermits, to serve as their priest.

Here at last Anthony was happy. He had the simple life of service and devout prayer he had always dreamed of. He thought that this was what God had planned for him.

But God's ways are not our ways. One day he was invited to the ordination of a priest, and the person who was to give the homily was unable to come. The local Dominicans all said they had not had enough time to prepare. The Dominican Order is a French order of preachers, which is why Dominicans have the letters O.P. after their name, which stand for 'Ordre de Prêcheurs' or 'Order of Preachers'.

So Anthony was asked to preach, at very short notice, and he did. From then on his life changed yet again. His fine mind, the excellent teaching from the Canons of St Augustine and his own natural gift, made St Anthony an amazing preacher. After this first sermon, he was asked to preach far and wide and the humble life at the hermitage was over forever.

St Francis and St Anthony lived in difficult times. Many priests were not leading good lives and this caused scandal to the lay people. Many different Gospel-based groups sprang up to try to make those priests behave better, but often ended up by fighting them!

Also, there were the heresies of the day: a 'heretic' is somebody who does not accept all of a belief system and changes parts of it to suit his ideas. Jesus founded the Catholic Church, and his teachings come down to us both through the Tradition of the early Church before the Gospels were written and later from Holy Scripture, which records this Tradition. In Christianity, a heretic is one who does not accept all these teachings of Jesus and changes or leaves out some parts.

The great heresy of that time was 'Manicheism' (Manni - kay - ism) but it went under other names as well. This was a heresy dating from the time of St Augustine of Hippo (See earlier story about him), which had come back again.

It taught that there was not one God but two, a good one and a bad one. The good god created the pure spiritual things and the bad god made all material things. The material things mean things in the world, which we see and touch, and even people themselves. These heretics believed that all 'matter' was evil. Therefore they could not believe that Jesus Himself could be present in the Blessed Sacrament, because bread and wine were material things that must have come from the bad god.

St Anthony felt very sorry for them, as he could think of nothing worse than not to be able to receive Our Lord in Holy Communion. His sermons were all about the great need for the Sacrament of Penance, and for the Blessed Sacrament. Although he realised that we often abuse the good things God gave us, he reminded people that in Genesis, the first book of the Bible, God created the world including all matter, and 'saw that it was good'.

That St Anthony was the worker of an amazing number of miracles is very clear, but it is hard to be sure in each case what is legend and what is historically true.

Here are some of the most interesting stories:

Once, St Anthony went to preach in a town called Rimini, where all the people believed in the heresy that all matter was evil. The town leaders ordered the people to ignore St Anthony. So he just walked around praying and nobody came near him.

Then he went to the river and began to preach to the fish. Suddenly rows of different fish poked their heads out of the water like a huge crowd of people listening to a sermon. Even fish that were natural enemies were side by side listening to him. This extraordinary event made the people come out of their houses and listen to St Anthony's preaching. The whole town converted back to the Catholic Faith.

Everywhere he went to preach, St Anthony brought people back to the Faith or made Catholics, who were still faithful, more devout. He became very well known. But, as it was with his divine master, Jesus, his success in preaching goodness made him enemies, who wanted to kill him.

Once, some enemies invited him into their home and poisoned the food they were going to give him. St Anthony knew this and reproached them for it. They reminded him of the Gospel where Jesus says that his disciples could eat even deadly poison and not die. But Jesus, when He was tempted by the devil during his forty days in the wilderness, had also said we must not put God to the test.

This put St Anthony into a difficult position, so he made the sign of the cross over the food and said that he was not trying to put God to the test but was eating the food because he wanted his host to return to the Catholic Church founded by Jesus. He then ate the food and was not harmed by it. The whole household and many of their friends put aside their heresy and returned to the Faith.

Another time, a band of trouble-makers came to listen to his sermon. But they were so moved by what Anthony said that they did not make any trouble. They were sorry for their sinful way of life and decided to change it. They all went to confession. The priest gave them all the same penance for their bad behaviour: that they should visit the tombs of the apostles twelve times before they died. Some did this and some did not. Those who did not had a miserable and early death, but those who did remain faithful lived a long and happy life. This story was told by an elderly man, when he had just come back from his twelfth visit to the tombs.

Plate 49: St Anthony and the Miracle of the Severed Foot

At another time, a young man went to confession to St Anthony and confessed that he had become so angry with his mother that he had kicked her. St Anthony was so shocked to hear this that he said that anyone who would kick their own mother deserved to have their foot cut off. He did not really mean this of course, but the young man was very simple and went back home and cut off his foot with an axe! The mother rushed to St Anthony screaming for his help. St Anthony went to their house, where the young man lay. He prayed for them, begged the help of God and then miraculously put the man's foot back on.

There is a rather sweet story, but although there were definitely many miracles, we cannot be certain whether this is fact or legend. After preaching on the Blessed Sacrament one day a man said to him that if his mule were to bow down in reverence to adore the Host, then he would believe that Christ was really present in the Sacrament.

So, the man starved his mule for three days. When St Anthony held up the Host, the man offered the mule a bag of food. The mule ignored the food and bent down on his knees before the Blessed Sacrament. The man came back to the Apostolic Faith.

Plate 50: St Anthony and the Mule

St Anthony was good at helping people who were depressed, and often sorted out marriage problems. There was a man who would not even hold his new-born baby son, because he thought he was not the father. St Anthony said to the baby, "I command you in the name of Jesus Christ true God and true man, born of the Virgin Mary, to tell me in a clear voice that all of us can hear, who is your father." The newborn baby looked directly at his father and said, "Behold, this is my father."

Much later, after the death of St Anthony, a heretic went with his friends into the basilica where the Saint was buried. He had a bloody handkerchief over his eye. He claimed that he was blind and asked all the people to pray that the saint would give him back his sight. He meant to jeer at them afterwards by taking the bandage off and tell them that he had never been blind anyway.

The joke backfired, because when he took off his bandage he found that he was blind. He and all his followers were so shaken by this that they decided to change their bad lives, put aside the heresy and return to the Faith. The man received his sight back after he had confessed his sins.

St Anthony had a gift for making people sorry without making them resentful. Despite all the miracle stories, he should be most admired and followed because of his humble use of his very fine mind and great learning. His miracles always made people sorry for their sins and decide to live a better life.

One day he wrote to St Francis, asking if he might teach theology, the study of God, to the young friars. St Francis was at first not keen to see his friars become educated. He just wanted them to remain poor and humble, preaching God by the example of the simple poverty of the Gospel.

The Pope, however, had just asked the two new orders, the Dominicans and the Franciscans, for help against the many heresies of the day. Many of the heretics were learned and the simple friars just did not know enough to argue with them. St Francis sent back this reply:

To my dearest brother Anthony, your brother Francis. I approve your plan to teach holy theology to the friars, as long as this study does not extinguish (put out) the spirit of prayer and devotion, as has been written in the Rule. May you be well.

A friend of St Anthony, the Abbot of Vercelli, said of him that what was true of St John the Baptist was true of him: he was a lamp that burned brightly. He so burned with love in his heart that it was visible for all to see.

St Anthony had often wondered whether Our Lady and St Joseph had offered pigeons or turtle doves at the presentation of Baby Jesus in the temple, as the Gospels do not tell us which. On the Feast of the Presentation, just as he was singing that part of the liturgy that speaks of the offering made to the temple, a pair of turtle doves flew over the reading desk where Anthony was singing. So he now knew that it was turtle doves that had been offered!

Plate 51: The Presentation of Jesus in the Temple

During the late Middle Ages, there were the Crusades and also Pilgrimages. This meant that people travelled across the world far away from their home. At home they could simply exchange goods, but the travelling made it necessary to have money in coins and notes like we do now.

Sometimes people needed money immediately, which they did not have at the time, but knew they would have later. Rich people then set up as money-lenders, who would then lend that money until an agreed date, when it was to be paid back. There was a charge for this service so that, when people paid back the sum they borrowed, there was an extra payment for being able to borrow the money in the first place. This extra payment is called 'interest' and it is how banks still work today.

However, sometimes, bad people would lend money at a very high rate of interest to poor people, who in the end were unable to pay and were put into prison. This is called 'Usury' and is forbidden by the Church.

St Anthony preached at the funeral of one of these greedy money-lenders and said that he should not be buried in holy ground because he was already in hell. He quoted Our Lord's words:

For where your treasure is there will be your heart (Matthew vi: 21).

The people opened up the man's side and found that his heart was missing. Later it was found in his treasure chest!

St Anthony also bilocated. That means that he was in two different places at once. Once, when he was preaching in one town, he remembered he was supposed to be reading a lesson in his community chapel. He stood silent for a while in front of the congregation, while at the same time he appeared to the friars in his chapel and recited the office.

Another time he was preaching in a church, when he was also needed to sing the Alleluia for his community. He put his hood over his head and paused in his homily. At the same time he was seen and heard singing the alleluia at his friary.

St Anthony became known as 'The Saint' in his lifetime. There was not enough room in the cathedrals for all those who would come to hear him preach, so much of his preaching was done in the town squares or open fields. He had to have a bodyguard to stop people with scissors from snipping off a part of his habit as a relic.

The years of travelling had made the malaria he had caught in Africa come back and St Anthony became very ill. Because the ground was damp in the hermitage where he was being looked after, they built him a house in a huge walnut tree.

One night the Count Tiso, on whose land it was, saw a very bright light coming from the tree house, and he went to look in. He found it hard to believe what he saw: St Anthony was holding the little Baby Jesus in his arms. St Anthony begged Count Tiso not to speak of this, and he did not do so until after the Saint's death.

Plate 52: St Anthony and Baby Jesus

Just after he died, aged only 36, Anthony paid a visit to his friend, the Abbot of Vercelli, who had a very sore throat. Vercelli was not surprised to see him, as he had not heard that he had died. St Anthony touched his throat and it was better straight away. When they looked for him to give him some food he had disappeared. Afterwards the Abbot discovered that the Saint was already dead when he had visited him.

As he was believed to be a saint in his lifetime, it took less than a year for the Pope, Gregory IX, to canonize him. Interestingly, although his home town of Lisbon had not yet had the news that he had been proclaimed a Saint, all the church bells started pealing on their own, and the people went wild with joy. Only later were they told that he had been canonized on that day.

St Anthony is also known for these three things:

1: 'St Anthony's Bread', which means that, when he has granted a favour to somebody, he wants that person to thank him by feeding the poor, or helping some charity to do so.

2: Protection against the Devil, by wearing a tiny piece of material on which is written the words:
    'Behold the cross of Christ. Flee O Enemy. The Lion of the Tribe of Judah has defeated you, the shoot of David. Alleluia, Alleluia!'

3: For finding lost things (including the Faith). Small children used to chant:
    'St Anthony, St Anthony, please look around.
    Something is lost that must be found'.

People through the ages have reported incredible stories of things being found, valuable cheques, keys rings etc, through the help of St. Anthony.

Most importantly we must remember St Anthony for his holiness, as he is described by Abbot Vercelli, filled like the Baptist with a light for all to see, his heart burning with love for God and the wish to serve Him.

St Anthony, Pray for us.

NOTE FROM THE EDITOR

My wife Nicole, known to many as Nicky, succeeded in completing the trio of 'From Granny with Love' books just before she died in July 2008.   The task of arranging their publication therefore fell to me.   Various factors have led to a slight delay in publication.   However, I hope that the intrinsic merits, in my not unbiased view, of her books will be unaffected by this delay.

This book is the first of the three books in the 'From Granny with Love' series and takes the reader through Confession and First Holy Communion. The second book, subtitled 'This World is not Enough', covers The Life of Jesus.   The third book, subtitled 'Remember, You only Live Twice', addresses Confirmation.

Nicky has included in each book a variety of stories, from both ancient and more recent times, which illustrate the exploits of people struggling to lead a Christian life.

To remain as true as possible to her writings, I have left unchanged most of her typescripts, only making minor amendments where that is clearly indicated by the changed circumstances.   She never had the chance to do a final editing and I have not been able to attribute every quotation, nor to track down the editions of all the books that she used.   I have also left her Bibliography and Acknowledgements largely as they were, as I have no way of knowing how to complete them.

One area which has been difficult has been the selection and placing of photographs within the text, as Nicky left few instructions as to which photographs she would like to be placed where.   On this, I am exceedingly grateful both to Father Bernard Davenport and also to Francis Phillips for their invaluable assistance, without which I would undoubtedly have been floundering.   May I also express my sincere gratitude to everyone who has suggested or contributed paintings or photographs for the plates.

May I say that I am not aware of having trodden on the toes of any copyright. Whilst I have made every effort to obtain the necessary permissions for all material used, there may have been inadvertent omissions or items for which, being no longer able to consult the author, I simply could not locate the source. May I therefore beg indulgence for any infringement that may unwittingly have taken place, which will of course be corrected in any future edition.

May I also express my sincere gratitude to everyone that Nicky mentioned in her Acknowledgements and to all those other people who she would have included in that list had she lived long enough to complete it.

Finally, I would like to add my personal thanks to all those who have so kindly helped her and me to enable her writings to see the light of day.

Peter Hall

September 2009

THE COLOUR PLATES

Plate: Title:	Artist or Source
1: Jesus, I am Sorry for my Sins	Kate Sherwood
2: Baptism	Fr Bernard Davenport
3: The Last Supper	Leonardo da Vinci, by Giacomo Rafaelli
4: Moses with the Ten Commandments	English Mission Hospital, Jerusalem, by 'Dmy'
5: The Good Shepherd	Bernhard Plockhorst, by Phrood
6: The Last Supper	Andrea del Castagno
7: The Consecration of the Host	Yousuf Karsch
8: Pope Benedict XVI gives Holy Communion	CIEL UK
9: The Crucifixion	Andrea Mantegna, by Dmitry Rozhkov
10: The Consecration of the Chalice	CIEL UK Mass, 2001
11: A Tabernacle	Unknown
12: Noah making a Sacrifice	Anton Koch
13: First Holy Communion	Fr Bernard Davenport
14: St John the Evangelist	Butler's Lives of the Saints
15: St Peter	Butler's Lives of the Saints
16: The Good Shepherd	Fratelli Bonella
17: The Sacred Heart	Servitiu
18: The Expulsion of Adam and Eve from the Garden of Eden	Masaccio, by Morgoth
19: The Departure of Abraham	Jozsef Molnar, by Csanady
20: The Baby Jesus	Benvenuto Tisi, by Bejnar
21: The Lamb of God	Cathedral of Our Lady, Los Angeles by Andreas Praefcke
22: Cardinal Lustiger	George Strickland
23: The Monstrance	Père Claudiomar
24: Corpus Christi Procession, Campos, Brazil	Père Claudiomar
25: Our Lady – Queen of Heaven	Diego Velazquez, by Escarlati
26: Child praying	Fr Bernard Davenport
27: Children kneeling in Prayer	Emile Munier, by Mattes

28: Jesus as a Child   Bartolome Esteban Murillo
                                           by Reaverflash

29: St Anthony of Padua   Prayer Card from
                                           Messenger of St Anthony

30: St Padre Pio   Saint Pio of Pietrelcina Centre UK
31: St Catherine Laboure   Holy Card
32: The Return of Edmund Campion   Maureen Readings
33: Our Lady of Walsingham   Holy Card
34: Pope John Paul II   Holy Card
35: St Cecilia   Artist unknown in the collection
                                           of Jane Ewart

36: Dedication of St Agnes to Jesus   Andreas Praefcke
37: St Sebastian's Martyrdom   Albrecht Altdorfer
38: St Elisabeth-Rose, Abbey of Rozoy-le-Vieil
                                           Eugene Vandebeulque
39: St Felicity and Perpetua   Gaetan Poix,
                                           Church of Notre Dame de Vierzon
40: St Augustine of Hippo   Butler's Lives of the Saints
41: Pope Gregory sends St Augustine to England
                                           by Gryffindor, from
                                           Westminster Cathedral

42: St Thomas Aquinas   Butler's Lives of the Saints
43: St Francis singing to the Birds   Unknown
44: San Damiano Crucifix   Sevenhoven
45: St Clare of Assisi   Butler's Lives of the Saints
46: St Francis taming the Wolf   Peter Hall by kind permission of
                                           Maureen Readings
47: Nativity Scene   Beato Angelico, by Twice
48: St Anthony of Padua   Ravensburg Liebfrauenkirche,
                                           by Andreas Praefcke
49: St Anthony and the Miracle of the Severed Foot
                                           Titian
50: St Anthony and the Mule   Domenico Beccafumi
51: The Presentation of Jesus in the Temple
                                           Hermetiker, Church of Gutenzell
52: St Anthony and Baby Jesus   Chris Caldwell, St Anthony
                                           Medical Centre, St Louis

ACKNOWLEDGEMENTS
FOR
PERMISSIONS TO USE THE COLOUR PLATES

Our most grateful thanks are due for the kind permissions that have been granted by the following copyright holders of specific plates:

With grateful appreciation to:

Plate 1:	Mrs Kate Sherwood.
Plates 2, 13, 26:	Fr Bernard Davenport
Plate 7:	The Executors of the Yousuf Karsch estate
Plates 8, 10:	Ciel UK
Plate 16:	Fratelli Bonella and CBC Newry
Plate 22:	George Strickland, Directions to Orthodoxy
Plates 23, 24:	Père Claudiomar, Campos, Brazil
Plate 29:	Messenger of St Anthony, Padua
Plate 30:	The Saint Pio Centre
Plate 32:	Mrs Maureen Readings
Plate 35:	Mrs Jane Ewart
Plate 38:	Eugene Vandebeulque

Plate Numbers: 3; 5; 6; 9; 12; 18; 19; 20; 21; 25; 27; 28; 37; 47; 49; 50:
These images are all in the public domain and our most grateful thanks go to the artists who are named, where known, in the preceding list of plates.

Plate Numbers: 17; 36; 41; 44; 51:
These images are used on the basis of a Creative Commons Attribution Share-Alike 3.0 licence, with our most grateful thanks to the originators of these images.

Plate Numbers: 4; 39; 48; 52:
These images are used on the basis of a Creative Commons Attribution 3 Unported licence, with our grateful thanks.

SELECT BIBLIOGRAPHY

A Dictionary of Saints
        Donald Attwater

The Oxford Dictionary of Saints
        David Hugh Farmer

Demain La Chrétienté
        The Rt Rev Dom Gérard Calvet O.S.B.

The Message of Assisi
        Chris Simpson S.F.O.

Anthony of Padua
        Fr Jude Winkler O.F.M.

Note: This bibliography remained unfinished at the author's death.

ACKNOWLEDGEMENTS

Mrs Marguérite Josée Turle

Fr Bernard F. Davenport

Fr Andrew Wadsworth

Fr J. Bertram Cong. Orat.

Mrs Francis Phillips

Miss Merryn Howell

Mrs Mary Carey

Mr Michael Carson-Rowland

Mrs Rosemary Daniel

Mrs Rosaline Dusting

Mrs Marianne Machin

Miss Grace Reading

Mrs Maggie Sherwood

Mrs Maria-Cecilia Woolgar

Miss Cecily Perry Robinson

FINAL READERS

Mrs Mary Carey

Mrs Francis Phillips